Fishing Bamboo

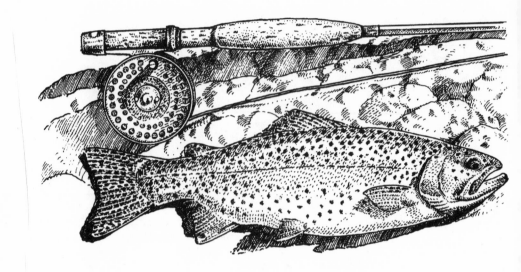

Fishing Bamboo

John Gierach

Illustrations by Glenn Wolff

The Lyons Press

Printed in the United States of America

Design and composition by Rohani Design, Edmonds, Washington

10 9 8 7 6 5 4 3 2 1

Library of Congress Cataloging-in-Publication Data

Gierach, John, 1946–
        Fishing Bamboo / John Gierach
                p.   cm.
        Includes bibliographical references.
        ISBN 1-55821-591-3 (cloth) ISBN 1-58574-233-3 (paperback)
        1. Fishing rods. 2. Bamboo. 3. Fly Fishing—Equipment and supplies.
    1. Title
    SH452.G54 1997
    668.7'9—dc21   97-10034
                                                                  CIP

"When you love something, you have the capacity to bore everyone about *why*—it doesn't matter why."

— John Irving

Contents

Acknowledgments

I COULDN'T HAVE WRITTEN this book without the help of my friends, and I *wouldn't* have written it without their encouragement. I don't dare try to list all the rod makers, dealers, collectors, and fishermen who have helped me out over the years by showing me and sometimes selling me rods, feeding me technical and historical information in terms simple enough for me to understand, and passing on their strongly held and sometimes conflicting opinions.

I do owe special thanks to A. K. Best and Ed Engle for years of great fishing and great talk about bamboo rods—among other things. Thanks to Pat Leonard and Mike Price for looking over the manuscript (both claimed not to be editors, then went on to do some pretty hard-nosed editing) and to my two bamboo rod gurus, John Bradford and Mike Clark, who have helped me to form some strongly held and conflicting opinions of my own.

— JOHN GIERACH
Lyons, Colorado

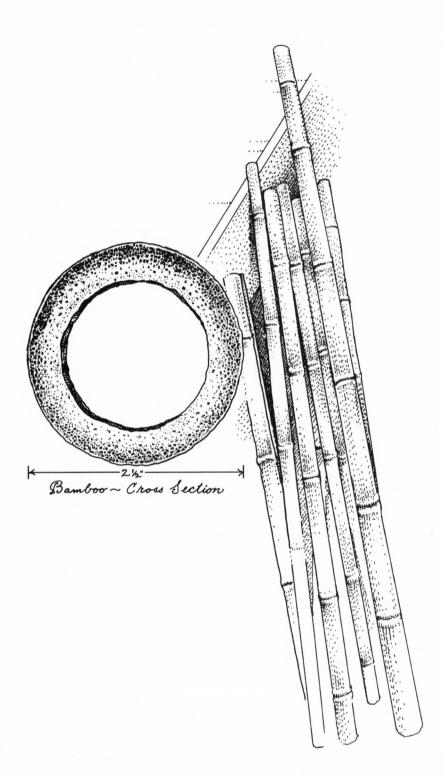

Bamboo ~ Cross Section
2½"

1

Fishing Bamboo

YOU SHOULD UNDERSTAND that I'm writing this not as an expert on split-bamboo fly rods but as an enthusiast with some opinions. In *Live Water*, Tom McGuane tells about asking his so-called Uncle Ben, "Was my father a good fisherman?" Uncle Ben smiles and says, "No Tommy, he was not. But no one loved it more." That's how I am with bamboo rods. Plenty of people know more about them, cast them better, and have seen more of them, but no one loves them more.

At first, it was probably as much an accident of timing as anything else. When I started fly fishing, the standard fly rod was fiberglass, but there were lots of fly fishers who thought bamboo rods were still the best, or who at least talked and wrote about them with reverence. Those fishermen included some heavyweights like Ernest Schwiebert and Arnold Gingrich, as well as any number of crusty old guys you never heard of.

Graphite rods were starting to show up then (it was the 1970s: the era of disco and Watergate) and some outrageous claims were being made for them, usually having to do with unbelievable casting distances, monumental strength, and the huge fish you'd catch if you'd only embrace the new technology. Advertisers believed then—and still believe now—that if you just showed a picture of a guy holding a big enough fish, you could claim he caught it because of the brand of underwear he had on and people would run right out and buy it.

Most of the fishermen I knew then considered these graphite things to be experimental toys for saltwater headhunters, but in the early 1970s Al McClane said he thought graphite would "replace fiberglass during the next decade." Which is pretty much what happened, at least in the mass market.

Of course, that was the same market that said fiberglass had "replaced" bamboo after the Second World War and, for that matter, that spinning had replaced fly fishing. But then considering the simpleminded way businessmen view reality and the glassy-eyed way some folks just go along with it, I guess that was true enough. I mean, people tend to get the politicians and the fishing tackle they deserve.

It may have been another coincidence, but about the time I got into fly fishing I also decided there should be one thing in my life that was of high quality—one thing because that's probably all I'd ever be able to afford—and it wasn't going to be clothes or cars or houses or jobs or pedigreed animals or fine books or fine liquor or antique furniture or matching china or snakeskin cowboy boots; it was going to be fly rods. And the best fly rods were bamboo, period.

Back then I made the same mistake about bamboo that others were beginning to make about graphite: I thought there was some magic in the material itself and that any rod made from the stuff would be wonderful. The H. L. Leonard Rod Company was still in business then and still making bamboo rods; so were Orvis, R. L. Winston, and Thomas & Thomas, plus a bunch of independent rod makers who somehow hadn't gotten the news that bamboo had been replaced. But I was working for pretty close to the minimum wage, so naturally my first bamboo rod was the cheapest one I could find at the time: an 8-foot, three-piece, 7-weight Ed M. Hunter bought new over the counter at Dave Cook's Sporting Goods in Denver.

It was the cheapest one I could locate, but it was still a little on the expensive side. Over time I'd get used to that. In the last twenty-five years or so I've spent more than I could really afford on bamboo fly rods, although I can't bring myself to say I've spent more than I should have. I mean, it was my money and my decision: If I had better fly rods than I did jobs, clothes, or pickup trucks, so be it. I was exercising my passion as well as I could, and I was damned lucky to *have* a passion.

I didn't know it then, but that particular Hunter was made by DeBell in Denver. Before that the Phillipson Rod Company had made rods under the trade name of Ed M. Hunter and they were actually pretty good, but the one I got was a club—although I didn't realize it until I got my hands on a sweet little 8-foot, 5-weight Granger Victory with a quick, graceful, forgiving action. It was magnificent, and the Granger, being an old, used fishing pole, was cheaper than the new Hunter had been. As I remember it, I unloaded the Hunter, bought a Pflueger Medalist reel, and about broke even. Then I went on to fish the Granger so hard I eventually had to get it refinished. I still have it.

I think that was pretty much it. The first really good fly rod I ever owned was bamboo, and it was at a time when that was considered only slightly unusual for someone my age. After all, every article you saw in those days about getting started in fly fishing still gave you three choices of fly-rod materials: fiberglass, graphite, and bamboo. Glass was cheap and good, graphite was new and high tech, but bamboo was still the benchmark.

On the other hand, my first really *crappy* fly rod was also bamboo, so I accidentally started out with a nice perspective on the whole business.

Some of my oldest fishing friends also use bamboo. Ed Engle and I got into writing, fly fishing, and bamboo fly rods more or less together and, for better or worse, have stuck with all three.

The first time I went fishing with A. K. Best, he strung up a beautiful little 5-weight Heddon President as if it was just another fishing pole. We got along in lots of other ways, too, but there was something about both of us pulling bamboo rods from dented old tubes that started things out on the right foot.

Not long after that A. K. introduced me to John Bradford of Fort Worth, Texas, a fine rod maker and one of the best rod restoration men around. John refinished some of our rods, including A. K.'s great Heddon, which came back looking better than it had new.

When I heard there was a guy named Mike Clark who was making bamboo rods right down the road from me, I looked him up, started hanging around his workshop, and we became friends. I learned most of what I know about rods from Mike, and I got the third rod he made professionally, after quite a few years of driving heavy equipment full time, learning rod making part time, and using failed blanks for fuel in the woodstove in his primitive shop.

He actually didn't start out to make rods for a living, he just wanted a bamboo rod and, being the self-sufficient, hands-on type, he thought it would be cheaper and more fun to make one than to buy one. But then people started offering him money, which has a way of changing everything. Now Mike makes rods full time and is back-ordered for well over two years. With the typical rod-maker crankiness, he says he guesses it beats driving a bulldozer.

My first Mike Clark rod was an 8½-foot, two-piece 5-weight that I still fish. I told him I wanted a powerful, authoritative 5-weight that could also handle light tippets and be capable of some delicacy: you know, a rod that would let you fish #22 Blue-winged Olives on 7X in a moderate gale. It does that. I have no idea how, but then that's why I'm writing about bamboo rods instead of making them.

A. K. liked mine so much, he ordered one just like it. My serial number is 833: the third rod Mike made in 1983. A. K.'s is 841: the first rod in 1984. (Some makers number their rods more for their own information than yours.)

For the record, Mike and I are not in business together—if we were, I wouldn't be as quick to talk him into closing the shop for a few days to go fishing—but he does make three models of rod with my name on them. There's the 8½-foot 5-weight and an identical 6-weight he calls the Gierach/Best Special Tapers because A. K. and I both use them and like them, and there's the 7-foot, 9-inch 5-weight Gierach Signature, complete with the full intermediate wraps that I asked for and that Mike gripes about every time he makes one.

In return I have one of each of those rods to fish with, plus the shot to the ego every time another one goes out the door, which seems like a pretty good deal to me. Over the years a handful of people have told me I should get more out of it than that—usually the same people who don't know what the hell

I'm talking about when I say I'd rather keep a good friend than get a few bucks a pop on fly rods.

A lot of my friends fish graphite, too, and I don't hold it against them, but it's surprising how often bamboo rods just sort of materialize. Susan Peterson has a 7½-foot Charlie Jenkins that comes out for special occasions. Roy Palm has been known to fish little creeks with a 3-weight Gary Howells. When A. K., Ed, Mike, and I were camped at Roy's place on the Frying Pan River last September, Roy's lawyer dropped by, the talk turned to rods, and he ran out to the car to get his Todd Young parabolic—the first one I'd ever seen—and so on.

Oddly enough, I ran into a fair number of people with bamboo rods in Alaska a few years ago. Up there, where your average fly fisher chunks lead on an 8-weight graphite most days, it seemed like half the fishermen I met had a little bamboo dry-fly rod tucked away for grayling.

At Iliaska Lodge in Iliamna, Ted Gerken had a collection of Thomas & Thomas limited-edition bamboo rods on the walls—unfished and under glass. Still, he was surprised that I was fishing for sockeyes with a 9½-foot, 8-weight Jim Payne light salmon rod. He was amazed at the weight of the thing (something like 9½ ounces fitted with the detachable fighting butt, slightly over a pound with a Peerless #6 salmon reel) and although he was too polite to say anything, I got the impression he thought I must be trying to prove something.

I was, of course, if only that at the time the lovely old Payne had cost me no more than I'd have paid for a comparable new graphite from any one of half a dozen companies.

Anyway, I have a copy of Ted's book, *Gamble at Iliamna*, with an apparently cryptic inscription that reads: "To John Gierach and his strong right arm."

By the time I got into them, bamboo fly rods had bred a subculture of professional and amateur rod makers, dealers in used rods, rod restoration people, collectors, historians, and fishermen that the larger culture of fly fishers seems more or less unaware of. I say that based on the two most common questions I hear about bamboo rods: "Aren't they all antiques?" and "Where the hell do you *get* these things?"

I can't say how many working bamboo rod makers there are in the United States right now. About ten years ago I was researching a magazine article on bamboo rods and I asked Hoagy Carmichael, coauthor with the great Everett Garrison of *A Master's Guide to Building a Bamboo Fly Rod* and a fine rod builder himself, how many rod makers there were. I told him I'd dug up twenty-eight. He said that if I meant people who were selling their rods more or less regularly and maybe even making all or part of a living at it, that was probably about right, but that he knew of over a hundred other craftsmen working in basements and garages on evenings and weekends, some of whom were turning out excellent (though little-known) work and, not unimportant, "helping to keep the craft alive."

As near as I can tell, the number of professional bamboo rod makers has remained about the same over the last decade— although the personnel have changed a little—but the number of amateurs, hobbyists, part-timers, beginners, or whatever you want to call them has grown.

At this writing, Garrison and Carmichael's *Master's Guide* has gone back into print from Meadow Run Press—it's been the bible of the craft since it was first published in 1977—and there are several other books in print on making or restoring bamboo rods, not to mention profiles of well-known rod makers and companies, reproductions of old catalogs, and of course Martin Keane's standard *Classic Rods and Rodmakers*. The last time I checked, *Trout Tackle—Two*, a reprint of the fly-rod section of Ernest Schwiebert's two-volume magnum opus, *Trout*, was out of print. There's even a magazine "for those who make and appreciate the split bamboo fly rod." It's called *The Planing Form*, edited by Ron Barch in Hastings, Michigan. Its circulation is around five hundred, with subscribers in the United States, Canada, Europe, Australia, South America, and Japan.

Ed Engle has been profiling bamboo rod makers in his "Cane Currents" column in *The Angler's Journal* for a couple of years now and he says he hears from or about more all the time. The same thing happened to me when I did that article ten years ago. In the weeks after it was published, half a dozen rod makers called and said, "Why didn't you put me in there?" and I had to say, "Because I didn't know you existed until this very moment."

Still, most fly fishers can tell you the names of more dead bamboo rod makers than live ones—people like Everett Garrison, Jim Payne, and Pinky Gillum—for the same reason they know about artists like Picasso and Rembrandt, that is, not so much for the quality of the work as for the horrifying prices collectors pay for it. That's why, when most fly fishers hear about a contemporary maker whose name sounds vaguely familiar, like Walt Carpenter, Ron Kusse, or Bob Summers, they'll ask, "Is he still alive?"

Someone once said of the poet Allen Ginsberg that he made it by selling poetry to people who don't *read* poetry. You could probably say something like that about bamboo rod makers.

One of the most common misconceptions about bamboo rods is that they're incredibly delicate. Jack Ohman picked up on that in one of the great cartoons in his book *Fear of Fly Fishing*. There's a rod on the wall in a glass case with three brass plaques hanging under it that read:

CANE ROD

DO NOT TOUCH

EVER

In the accompanying text, Ohman says, "Who wants to fish with something they're afraid to touch? Fishing with a cane rod is like playing rugby in your grandmother's sitting room."

By the way, some aficionados will yell at you if you call bamboo "cane," although I'm not one of them. What we're talking about here, they'll explain, are rods made from split *Arundinaria amabilis* 'McClure', commonly called Tonkin bamboo in America and Tea Stick bamboo in China. There are many other species of bamboo in the world, all of which are vastly inferior for fly rods, and all of which you can call cane if you want.

There are people like that in the world of bamboo rods: accuracy freaks who'll bust your chops over any little detail. You get used to that and maybe even come to appreciate it—after all, some of these guys really know their stuff—but nine times out of ten you can get away with saying "cane" or "split cane" without getting lectured about it.

You do see a fair number of broken bamboo rods and, yes, they do traditionally come with a spare tip, but most injuries to bamboo rods come from falls on rocks, getting tangled between boats and docks, getting slammed in screen doors and car doors, and being stepped on by clumsy fishing partners: the same kind of things that have snapped fly rods since the dawn of history.

Just the other day I saw a nice old F. E. Thomas salmon rod with a freshly broken tip. When I asked the guy how he did it, he said he had to quickly get out of the way of a brown bear on the Brooks River in Alaska. When it was all over, the tip was broken. He doesn't remember how it happened and he doesn't really care; he's just happy to be alive. In a case like that, as in most cases, the only difference between a bamboo and a graphite rod is, the bamboo can sometimes be fixed.

Actually, there's another difference: The bamboo rod has a spare tip, so you can keep fishing.

When graphite rods have been around continuously for over a century, you'll see just as many busted ones—probably more, since graphite is more brittle than bamboo and, by all rights, should also come with spare tips. In fact, there are lots of people, including me, who are the second and even third owners of good old bamboo fly rods that are still in regular use with no end in sight.

Mike fields that question a lot: "Aren't they awfully easy to break?" Rod makers like to point out that Tonkin bamboo does in the wild what it does in a fly rod—40-foot stalks of it bend in the strong winds and then snap back straight—and that bamboo has a higher tensile strength than steel. I've seen Mike grab the butt section of an unwrapped blank off the rack, throw it on the floor, and walk the length of it in hiking boots, while explaining that if it was a hollow graphite shaft it would be crushed. The customer gasps, Mike grins, and the point is made.

Another question I hear a lot is, "Okay, why is bamboo better than graphite?" and sometimes it's put just like that, in a kind of challenging tone. After all, most new bamboo rods cost more than most new graphites, and in a consumer-driven society, people naturally assume that means they're supposed to be better, so they want proof, or at least a good sales pitch.

Actually, bamboo *isn't* necessarily better than graphite, nor is graphite better than bamboo. They're just two materials that make two different kinds of rod.

Someone who's fished graphite for the last twenty years will probably say bamboo rods are too slow and heavy. To me, graphites feel too fast and light. It seems to me that the just noticeably slower casting stroke of bamboo is more charitable. I mean, it absorbs minor casting flaws instead of magnifying them. You'll sometimes hear fishermen say it takes a real expert to cast a bamboo rod well, but I think it's just the opposite: Your timing can be less than perfect or you can get tired and sloppy and a good bamboo rod will want to correct for it.

I was talking to Vince Zounek about that the other day. Vince is a fly-casting instructor and he said that sometimes, when he has a student who just can't quite get the timing of the cast right or can't feel the rod load, he'll hand him a bamboo rod and the light will come on. Bamboo just seems to be the more natural, accessible material for fly casting.

Ed once said he thought graphite rods were designed to *shoot* line, while bamboo rods were made to *cast* line, and I thought that was a nice distinction. I think a good bamboo rod feels alive and friendly, while a good graphite certainly feels efficient.

I also appreciate the extra weight of bamboo, especially in shorter, lighter rods. Manufacturers can't say enough about how light their graphite rods are, but to me that weightlessness is irritating. I can't feel them load and I'm always looking behind me to see what the line is doing on the backcast.

I think the weight of a bamboo fly rod acts like the weight of a hammerhead: It helps rather than hurts; magnifies the leverage; telegraphs the loading of the line down to the hand so I can feel what's going on; seems to do more of the work while I do less. We're not talking about much weight here, either. The difference between 8½-foot, 5-weight dry-fly rods made of bamboo and graphite is maybe 2 ounces: hardly enough to whine about.

Of course, raving about and sometimes even lying about light weight is a tradition that started with bamboo rod makers. Not that long ago, fly rods were designated by length and weight—rod weight, not line weight—so you'd buy yourself an 8½-foot, 5-ounce rod, on which you'd probably end up casting an HDH (or double-taper 6) silk line. To make a rod sound lighter, some rod makers would weigh just the blank, before the grip, reel seat, ferrules, guides, wraps, and varnish went on. That meant you could buy that 5-ounce rod, weigh it at home on a good scale, and find that it actually came in at 5½ or even 5¾ ounces. I don't know for sure, but I suspect that kind of thing still goes on. It probably amounts to a harmless little advertising scam, but Ralph Nader should still be alerted.

I've had much better luck striking and playing large fish on light tippets with bamboo—on those rare occasions when I *do* strike and play large fish. The live, natural fiber just seems to cushion things better, but then there's also enough backbone in most good rods to let you put the wood to a big fish.

People still say that. It sounds so much better than "putting the high-modulus graphite to him."

If you must nymph fish with weight on the leader (I know I must at times), a bamboo rod lobs the rig a little more grace-fully—but don't ever tell a rod maker he builds a nice lead rod.

I've heard people say a bamboo rod is more accurate than a graphite. I'd like to believe that, but I don't. Casters are accurate, not rods.

I've had this discussion quite a few times and, believe me, it goes on until the fire has burned down to coals: Okay, graphite is probably better for distance, assuming the fisherman using it is a decent distance caster. But then if he *is* good at longer ranges, he can probably get what he needs out of a bamboo—as long as he's not afraid to use it. (The people who say bamboo lacks power are usually the same ones who think they're easy to break, so they cast them the same way they'd handle a thousand-year-old vase.)

One fisherman will say, "Well, at least in the longer lengths, bamboo is just too damned heavy."

Another will say, "Yeah, you're right, not everyone is man enough to handle a big rod."

And so on.

The fact is, a good rod of any material—with the possible exception of tubular steel—will work just fine in most normal, freshwater fishing situations as long as the person holding it knows how to fish. If you can find one of the rare fiberglass holdouts, he'll tell you that quality glass has some of the best virtues of both bamboo *and* graphite, and he'll be right.

Bamboo just attracts a different kind of fisherman: Most of us are suckers for tradition and nostalgia, we like things that are handmade, prefer wood to plastic, tend to describe rods in humanistic rather than military terms, and are generally suspicious of new technology, which, more often than not, costs twice as much and works half as well as the old technology. We may not always spend as much time sitting on the bank listening to the birds sing as we do fishing, but we think we should.

We may not be dry-fly purists, but we'd like to be when we grow up.

We enjoy being part of an underground where rumors of new rod makers and photocopied used-rod lists circulate through the old, slow U.S. mail, and it's fun to be thought of as a little bit crazy even by other fly fishers, most of whom don't have much room to talk.

In a world where most days you have to settle for cheap merchandise made by robots and sold by surly zombies, some of us consider it an act of defiance to own something made by a dedicated craftsman who may well be working as much for love as money and who's proud enough of his work to sign it. If there's one legitimate criticism of synthetic rods, it's that they've killed too much of that kind of craftsmanship.

A fair number of us remember when bamboo was the standard when it came to fine fly rods and we're still not convinced that graphite isn't just a fad. Younger bamboo nuts seem to have the same perspective. They probably came by it from reading some old books or falling in with the wrong crowd.

Some fly fishers who eventually get into bamboo still see it as a kind of technical step up. After all, good bamboo rod fishermen are known to throw long, lovely, accurate casts and catch the hell out of fish, so you have to think casting one of these things is more than just a sensual experience informed by tradition. But then just as many consider it a step off to the side and say things like, "Well, if casting graphite is like typing an invoice on a word processor, casting bamboo is like writing a letter to a friend with a fountain pen."

For most of us, it's probably a little of both. Charlie Jenkins, the Denver rod maker, once told me that half of what people are buying when they get one of his rods is the idea of the lone craftsman down in the basement with his glasses pulled down on his nose, handmaking their rod. That's true, but then the other half is a really good fly rod. Even among those of us who are real pushovers, the romance won't kick in if the rod doesn't work.

I guess I'd like to explain my own fascination with bamboo rods a little more concisely—if only to satisfy my own curiosity—but apparently the best I can do is sort of sniff around the edges of it. I will say that when I'm casting any good rod I'll keep thinking, Jeez, this is really nice, but when I cast a *great* rod, I'll forget about it altogether and just fish brilliantly. The handful of truly great fly rods I've ever cast have all been made of bamboo.

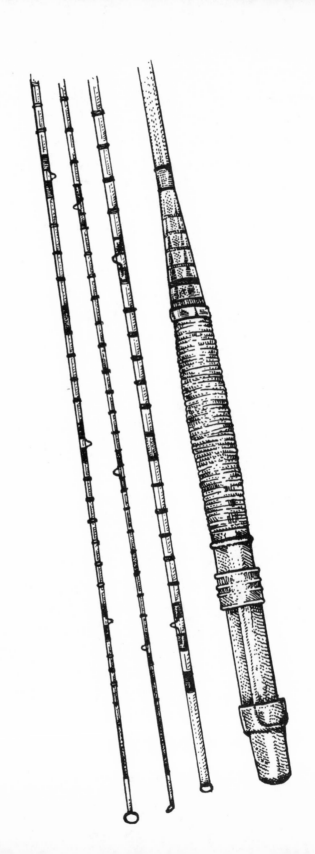

2

A Brief History

ONCE UPON A TIME, all fly rods were made of
solid wood: first woods from England, then different
woods from all over the British Empire. The way I see
it, the British Empire was established for no other reason than to
get rare wood for fly rods and exotic feathers for salmon flies, but
that hasn't been widely accepted by historians yet.

Fishermen agonized about this, as they've always done about
everything. There were dozens of different kinds of wood that
were commonly used in rods either by themselves or in combi-
nations, including whole—that is, unsplit—bamboo. You might
have wanted a rod with a butt section of hazel and a tip of black-
thorn or juniper. Another fisherman would have liked a butt of
fir and a tip of yew or cane and another might have wanted all
lancewood or greenheart—and you'd all probably have been
willing to argue about it.

"Rent and glued-up" bamboo first turned up as tip sections
on otherwise solid-wood rods, maybe because it was hard to

find whole pieces of it that were thin enough—although that's just a guess. These sections were usually made of three or four glued strips with the corners sanded round to match the rest of the rod shaft. There were also tips with alternating strips of wood and bamboo and tips built backward by modern standards, that is, with the enamel part of the bamboo on the inside instead of the outside.

By the mid-1800s, Charles F. Murphy, E. A. Green, Samuel Phillippe, and his son, Solon, had all built fly rods with at least some of their sections made from split bamboo. The angling historians I've read don't quite agree on who made the first complete six-strip split-bamboo rod, but it's probably safe to say fly rods made entirely of split bamboo had shaken themselves out of the workshops of the American Industrial Northeast at least by the early years of the Civil War.

It *is* clear that Murphy, Green, and the Phillippes knew each other and that they were all eclectic craftsmen and tinkerers. Most of these early rods came from shops that turned out all kinds of things, from firearms to canoe paddles. For instance, Samuel Phillippe made rods, but he was primarily a gunsmith and, by all accounts, a pretty good violin maker. These men would have seen each other's rods and they might have exchanged information or compared notes in the guarded way of craftsmen in competition with one another.

I like to think I can picture that, if only because I've seen it happen a few times: once on a fishing trip with, among others, rod makers Mike Clark, Charlie Jenkins, and Bob Summers, and again when John Bradford and Mike got together one day in Mike's shop. Any good rod maker wants to brag a bit without giving anything away, and at the same time maybe sniff out a little secret or two without actually seeming to ask.

It's fun to watch, even if you don't know exactly what they're talking about.

By the late 1870s Hiram Leonard had established the H. L. Leonard Rod Company, invented a milling machine to cut tapered strips of bamboo, and patented the waterproof ferrule. By about 1880 or so he'd decided to leave the outsides of the bamboo splines flat instead of sanding them round, because the outside of the bamboo is where the strongest, most powerful fibers are. There were fishermen who thought the rods were ugly, but they must have gotten over it eventually.

Of course, split bamboo didn't replace solid wood overnight any more than fiberglass replaced bamboo a hundred years later. Lots of fishermen still preferred wood rods and lots of sporting goods outfits sold both bamboo and wood fly rods at least up into the late 1920s. A Horrocks-Ibbotson catalog from about that era says of its lancewood rods, "Other kinds of wood and bamboo have been tried, but many expert fishermen, both in this country and England, still cling to the lancewood rods as being the strongest, most durable and best, both for fly casting and bait fishing." That poignant bit about how some fishermen "still cling" to wood rods makes me think they were beginning to fade out by then.

If nothing else, wood rods were easy to produce, at least once the Industrial Revolution got going in the mid-1800s. You'd get your taper by feeding a single squared strip of wood into a doweling machine set to round and taper it at the same time: sort of like a giant pencil sharpener. Compared to milling six separate strips of bamboo to precise fractions of the finished taper, gluing them up, straightening them, and so on, making wood rods was quick and simple and the price reflected that. Even up into the 1920s, wood rods were often cheaper than split bamboo.

You'd have to talk to a rod maker or an angling historian about how many significant advances there have been in bamboo rod building in the last century and exactly what they were. There's actually a lot more agreement on the flops. Fred Divine's eight-strip rods didn't quite get it. Neither did rods wrapped entirely in silk from one end to the other. Divine made those, too. He said, "They are absolutely water proof and much stronger than the ordinary split bamboo rod." They were also heavy and had actions like buggy whips. Split-bamboo rods with steel cores were also a little on the heavy side, and so were double-built rods, which were basically one bamboo rod inside another.

The spiral bamboo rods built by Divine and Letcher Lambuth never quite got it, either, and around the First World War, Hardy in England made monstrosities like double-built rods with steel centers, rods with steel ribbing, and nine-sided rods.

It's true that a lot of that kind of thing went on in the early days of bamboo rods, and also that a lot of it was pure marketing. In his commentary to *Great Fishing Tackle Catalogs of the Golden Age*, edited by Samuel Melner and Hermann Kessler, Sparse Grey Hackle said of some of Hardy's weirder ideas that they were "worse than worthless 'selling points.'"

I think that's right, and I think the same can be said of a lot of modern tackle, but there was probably also an honest side to it. The kind of craftsman who'd end up making something like bamboo fly rods would just necessarily have a healthy curiosity about whether or not it could be done better, along with the confidence that if it could, he'd be as likely to do it as anyone else.

You don't see as much of that outrageous experimentation now that bamboo rod making has settled into being a traditional craft, but it never completely went out of style. It wasn't that long ago that Barry Kustin was making what amounted to double-built rods with graphite inside the bamboo. You couldn't tell that just by looking at them—in fact they were real pretty—but they didn't catch on.

The latest thing is the Hexagraph rod that's made by gluing sheets of graphite to hard foam, milling it into strips, gluing it up like bamboo, and, worst of all, painting it to *look* like bamboo. My opinion is, there are some things you just can't make plastic copies of, and even if you can, you shouldn't. I predict they'll eventually become just one more humorous footnote in fishing tackle history.

Along with all the dead ends, though, there were what you'd have to call breakthroughs in the history of rod building. The grips on fly rods were once made of turned wood or wrapped rattan. They were pretty, but wood was heavy and rattan tended to fall apart. In the late 1880s, cork grips started to show up on so-called "ladies' rods," and it wasn't long before they became standard.

Thomas Chubb made the first one-piece, all-metal, seamless reel seat in the early 1880s; in the early 1900s Charles Treadwell built the first modern screw-locking reel seat; in the 1930s E. C. Powell and Lew Stoner were working on the hollow bamboo rods that would eventually make both Powell and the R. L. Winston Rod Company famous—not to mention Gary Howells, who left Winston in the late 1960s to make rods under his own name; the C. F. Orvis Company started making impregnated rods in the mid-1940s; and so on.

It was also in the mid-1940s that Nat Uslan began making his five-sided bamboo rods. They never caught on in a big way, but they still have their followers. The same goes for the four-sided or "Quadrate" rods developed by William Edwards. Many fishermen think of them as curiosities, but those who like them *really* like them and I've been told not to make up my mind about four-sided rods until I try one made by Sam Carlson.

I've talked to all kinds of rod makers, dealers, and collectors about this, and no two have agreed on what the real milestones were. For instance, I like some of the impregnated rods, so I throw that in, but I've heard people sniff and say a proper split-cane fly rod is varnished, period. In those guys' lists, impregnation would be replaced by some obscure development in marine spar varnish.

But really, bamboo fly rods haven't changed all that much since Hiram Leonard. The glues and varnishes have gotten better, and the guides, ferrules, and reel seats have been improved. Rods have gotten shorter—early in the twentieth century, bamboo fly rods 10 and 11 feet long were pretty common—some new tapers have been developed as casting styles changed, and rods have just generally gotten lighter, quicker, and more refined. Still, the rods have looked more or less the same and been made in pretty much the same way for more than a hundred years.

For generations, split-bamboo rods were the standard fishing poles. Hundreds of thousands were made and many of those were mass-produced. A few of the production companies turned out some really excellent rods (virtually all of the Grangers and Phillipsons, and some of the Heddons, for instance), but the majority (like most of the rods from Montague, Bristol, and Horrocks-Ibbotson) were pretty poor. Collectors and rod restorers tell you the best you can say about a lot of them is that they were cheap and they got the job done— which isn't all bad, by the way.

Alongside the production makers were the craftsmen work-ing either alone or in small shops with a handful of employees. They didn't turn out as many rods as the bigger companies, and not all their rods were masterpieces, either, but those from the most skilled makers are considered to be among the best bamboo rods ever made.

A precious few of these guys seemed to come out of no-where. Not that long ago, every other book on fishing included rough directions for how to make your own split-bamboo fly rod, and I get the feeling that planing your own cane rod was once about as common as building up graphites from blanks and components is now.

But most of the now-famous rod builders worked for well-known makers, went on to start their own shops, and trained other makers in the great old tradition of craftsmanship. The pedigrees of some of these craftsmen read like Genesis—Hiram Leonard begat Ed Payne who begat Jim Payne—although often there are more twists and turns to it than that.

Actually, Edward Payne, Fred Divine, Eustis Edwards, Thomas Chubb, Fred E. Thomas, Hiram Hawes, and George Varney all learned or at least perfected their rod making working for Leonard.

Fred Thomas went on to run the F. E. Thomas Rod Com-pany that lasted until 1958, when Fred's son Leon sold the company to rod maker Sam Carlson, who later sold the Thomas beveling machine to Walt Carpenter. (Carpenter himself had earlier worked for both the H. L. Leonard Rod Company and the E. F. Payne Rod Company.) You can call Walt up right now and order one of his rods—if you don't mind waiting a while.

Thomas Chubb went off and built rods of his own, and when the Montague City Rod Company bought out Chubb around the turn of the century, Chubb's old colleague George Varney went to work for them and made some of their best rods. Sewell Dunton also worked at Montague, then went off to make rods under his own name, then retired and sold his shop in Greenfield, Massachusetts, to Thomas Dorsey and Thomas Maxwell (Tom Maxwell also once worked for the Leonard Company), who became the Thomas & Thomas Company. You can still call T&T and order a rod, too.

You can pick apart the history of bamboo rods like an old rug and find dozens of those long threads, the majority of which lead back to H. L. Leonard, or at least the Leonard Company, in one way or another. When people call Leonard the father of the bamboo rod, that's what they're talking about. And of course on the other end, Hiram Leonard saw and was certainly influenced by the rods of Murphy, Green, and the Phillippes, who probably saw their first examples of split-bamboo construction on English rods.

(By the way, Mark Aroner of Conway, Massachusetts—who worked at Thomas & Thomas and Leonard—is still making rods on the H. L. Leonard Rod Company beveler. As I said, it goes on and on like that.)

A lot of the new generation of rod makers got started with the Garrison and Carmichael book, A Master's Guide to Building a Bamboo Fly Rod, and I once suggested to Mike that maybe that would turn out to be the final break with the Leonard tradition. He said no. Turns out Everett Garrison learned his rod making from a hobbyist named Dr. George Parker Holden, who wrote his own landmark book, The Idyll of Split Bamboo, back in 1920, and who had been known to hang around the shop run by, you guessed it, Hiram Leonard.

Once you're really bitten by bamboo rods themselves, you'll begin to get more and more curious about their history. You'll pick it up in bits and pieces, and then later in bigger chunks when you decide to do a little reading. If nothing else, it'll begin to give you a sense of why some rods are so valuable to collectors. Part of it is quality and part of it is rarity, but there's also something else that's harder to put your finger on.

In *Classic Rods and Rodmakers*, there's the great story about Harold Steele (Pinky) Gillum seeing a customer abusing one of his rods on the stream. Supposedly Gillum took the man's reel off the rod, refunded his money on the spot, and repossessed the thing. Now that plastic rods are guaranteed for life against clumsiness and stupidity, a story like that about a famous, dead rod maker is worth another hundred bucks on the price of one of his rods.

Of course, every little piece of the historical puzzle will include a few rods you'd sure like to see, cast, and maybe even own. In that sense, ignorance can be bliss.

Rod collectors have been known to get pretty mystical about all this and when someone mentions a legendary rod maker, it's easy enough to picture him sitting in the lotus position on the banks of a Catskill trout stream channeling H. L. Leonard. You have to stop and remind yourself that, although these people were artisans and fishermen, most of them were basically making a living doing work, with all of work's normal frustrations. (The boring part of bamboo rod history has to do with all the bankruptcies, failed partnerships, and bad distribution deals.) And although these people were known for making fine fly rods, there was no particular mystique about them working with bamboo. In those days, that's just what fly rods were made of.

Of course, if you spend an afternoon with any rod maker it'll soon become obvious that this is a job—a good, honorable, satisfying job with a built-in excuse to go fishing, but still a job. I don't know why that seems important, but somehow it does.

I think the only real change in the bamboo rod market is that, in about the early 1950s, the low end dried up. The cheap, pounded-out-by-the-gross, works-in-a-pinch bamboo fly rods, not to mention the good but still affordable rods, are the ones that really *were* all but replaced by fiberglass.

There were a few holdouts like Paul Hightower at Pioneer Rods and Fred DeBell, who made moderate-quality, moderately priced bamboo rods up into the 1970s, but many of the companies that made affordable bamboo rods eventually either gave it up altogether or turned to glass—reluctantly or otherwise.

By all accounts, Bill Phillipson thought fiberglass was pretty neat, and his small company in Denver made some real nice ones. On the other hand, Jim Payne was said to disapprove of glass even though, through one of those strange detours you see in business, there are some glass rods with his name on them.

But then some of the bigger companies (R. L. Winston and Orvis, for instance) just kept turning out bamboo rods as if nothing much had happened, and so did a lot of independent rod makers. You'll hear that the Golden Age of bamboo fly rods lasted roughly from 1930 to 1960 and then at some point after that there was a Renaissance in bamboo. But if that's true, you have to wonder why the careers of so many fine modern bamboo rod makers somehow plodded ahead through the years when split-cane rods were supposed to be dead. I mean craftsmen like

Glenn Brackett at R. L. Winston, Per Brandin, Sam Carlson, Hoagy Carmichael, Walt Carpenter, Tom Dorsey, Gary Howells, Charlie Jenkins, Tom Maxwell, Bob Summers, and Bob Taylor, to name just a few alphabetically.

There was a noticeable drop in the overall number of bamboo rods built and sold in those years, but other than that the only things that really happened between the end of the so-called Golden Age and the beginning of the so-called Renaissance were, fly shops began to look more like boutiques, and top-of-the-line bamboo fly rods by the classic makers started to get seriously collectible, cranking up the price and throwing a turd in the churn for those of us who just wanted to fish them.

By now just about all new bamboo fly rods, whether they're from individual makers or companies, are pretty high-ticket items. I don't mean they're all good, just that they're all expensive. (I'll get into the whole price business later. It can be a painful subject, so I'm putting it off.) Still, the best of the new rods are probably the best ever made. They're the result of generations of experience, refinement, and trial and error, but with better glues and finishes.

I guess there was one other change, too. People who fish bamboo rods are now sometimes seen as a little snooty, where only a decade or two ago we were just thought to be folks who liked good fishing tackle. I can't say the ostentation isn't there at times because, like anything else that can be seen as sort of high tone, bamboo rods do attract their share of people who are wound too tight.

Now and then a fisherman will brag about his bamboo rod in terms of how rare it is, how much he paid for it, how much more than that it's worth now, and what guts he has to fish a museum piece—never mind how the thing casts. I've also heard a few pointlessly arrogant statements like, "I refuse to fish a classic rod that's been refinished."

Luckily, someone like that usually draws the same response from fellow bamboo types that he would from anyone else. Basically: "Isn't it a shame to see a nice old rod like that wasted on an asshole?"

I'll admit it now and then pains me if someone thinks I fish bamboo rods because I'm stuck up, but then I remind myself of an anonymous quote A. K. had tacked up over his fly-tying bench for years. It said, "When you start worrying about what other people think of you, it's time to go fishing."

Cross Section ⌐

3

Kinds of Rods

YOU CAN BREAK bamboo fly rods into categories in a couple of different ways. Some people like to think in terms of handmade versus production rods—or at least those two terms are tossed around a lot—and that calls up two mental pictures: as Charlie Jenkins said, "The lone craftsman down in the basement with his glasses pulled down on his nose," as opposed to rods being whanged out by the hundred in a factory. You want to think of a handmade rod as being built entirely by a single craftsman whose signature appears in black ink on the butt section, and a production rod as one that passes through lots of anonymous hands as it's built and that has a company name stamped on it.

Some of the famous old rod makers did work alone—Lyle Dickerson, Pinky Gillum, and Everett Garrison are probably the best known—and so do many of the modern ones. And, at least in the old days, some cheap rods were turned out by the carload in, if not exactly "factories," then at least pretty good-sized shops.

A lot of those mass-produced rods—not all, but a lot—were of pretty poor quality, so the term "production rod" is usually not considered to be a compliment. Many handmade rods were and are downright magnificent—not all, but many—but "hand-made" isn't a guarantee of quality any more than "production rod" necessarily means the thing is junk.

As I said, those two terms are used freely, but when you start picking away at the distinction, it turns out not to be so clear cut.

When we talk about Jim Payne rods, we mean the ones turned out by the E. F. Payne Rod Company shop in Highland Mills, New York, in the years after James Payne took over from his father, Edward, and, around 1916, began to make some real innovations in the design of Payne rods. This was a small shop and it's said that no one but Jim Payne ever varnished one of the rods, but there were several employees, some well-known rod makers among them, who, as Ron Barch said recently, "came to work every day with lunch boxes." Still, when most fishermen refer to Payne rods, they mean James, not Edward, and they mean the man, not the company.

Granger rods were originally designed by Goodwin Granger, who began making rods as a hobby about the time Jim Payne was taking over his father's rod shop. They were manufactured in Denver by the dozen or so employees of the Goodwin Granger Rod Company and, after 1946, by Wright & McGill under the trade name Granger. Most Granger rods were made after Goodwin's death in 1931 and many of the innovations in Grangers were the work of Bill Phillipson, so when the same fishermen talk about Granger rods, they mean the company, not the man.

Company names don't usually mean much, anyway, because there are too many of them stamped or written on rods made by individual craftsmen. Mike Clark's rods are made entirely by him, one at a time, but most of them are actually signed "SOUTH CREEK, LTD.," followed by Mike's initials.

John Bradford's rods come with his signature on the rod itself and a company name on the tube. The impressive-sounding J. A. Bradford Company is comprised of John and his cat.

The C. W. Jenkins Rod Company now consists of Charlie Jenkins and his son, Steve, which hardly puts them in a class with General Motors.

Fishermen and collectors even associate rods by the larger, more faceless companies with the master rod builders who were in residence at the time—even if they didn't build all the rods themselves—so a guy might brag about having not just a Leonard, but a Tom Maxwell–era Leonard, or a Wes Jordan Orvis, or a Lew Stoner R. L. Winston. The guy he's bragging to might say, "Well, that's nice, but of course my newer *Glenn Brackett* Winston is a better rod."

And then some people like to make the distinction between rods that are hand planed and rods made on a milling machine or beveler. Most bamboo rods since Hiram Leonard have been made of splines cut on some kind of milling machine. Jim Payne, F. E. Thomas, and lots of other big names used milling machines, and so do many of the makers working today.

But then there are also lots of rod makers who meticulously hand plane their splines using a planing form. Builders who work this way say it makes a difference: that hand planing follows the grain in the bamboo more closely, so you don't get fibers that are sawn off abruptly at the edges of the rod's flat splines. They say the action of a hand-planed rod is more fluid and that the method is more respectful of the material. A maker who hand planes his rods told me recently, "With a milling machine, the bamboo comes off in chunks and sawdust. With a plane it comes off in one slow curl."

Everett Garrison worked that way. In fact he perfected hand planing and was such a meticulous craftsman in every way that his rods are still held up as a kind of ultimate standard for attention to detail. Garrison went so far as to alternate the directions of his guide wraps to reduce the torque on the rod shaft. Sure, it's possible one little thing like that doesn't make enough difference to worry about, but Garrison is legendary for having done *everything* that way.

This gets to be a delicate point. Some say a handmade rod is one built entirely by a single craftsman, regardless of how he does it. Others say only a hand-*planed* rod is handmade. There are also some makers who split the difference by rough milling the splines and then finishing them by hand on a planing form or touching up milled splines with a plane, just to further confuse things.

I like Grangers a lot, but if you want to call them production rods, it's fine with me. I mean, they were turned out on milling machines in a shop with a dozen employees and most of the rods were made after Granger himself had died. Also, there were a hell of a lot of them made: thousands and thousands.

On the other hand, Everett Garrison's rods were all hand planed by the maestro himself on a planing form he designed, and, according to Martin Keane, he probably only made around seven hundred rods in his entire career.

When it comes right down to it, the difference between production and handmade rods is probably a useless distinction for fishermen, or one that only works at the far ends of the scale.

In fact, that's how a lot of people use the terms. A Montague or Horrocks-Ibbotson is called a production rod and a Gillum or a Garrison is said to be handmade, but an F. E. Thomas or an R. L. Winston is just a Thomas or a Winston, period.

For my money, if you walked into a workshop with a bamboo rod, asked who made it, and half a dozen people all said at once, "I split the cane," "I ran the beveler," "I glued the splines," "I wrapped the guides," and so on, you'd be holding a production rod. If, on the other hand, one guy puts down his coffee cup, turns down the radio, and says, "I did," then you've got a handmade rod, and I guess it doesn't matter to me whether he used a plane, a beveler, or a pocketknife.

Hell, I'd even look the other way if he had a neighborhood kid in there wrapping guides and sweeping up the bamboo shavings.

I *will* say I have a real soft spot for the idea of hand-planed rods because I appreciate that kind of thinking about craftsmanship, because I'm amazed at the skill it takes to work to tolerances of a thousandth of an inch with hand tools, because hand-planed rods take longer to make so there aren't as many of them, and, I guess, because they're just romantic as hell. There *is* a kind of mystique attached to this. That's probably why the magazine for bamboo rod makers is called *The Planing Form* instead of *The Milling Machine*.

As for whether or not it makes a difference, it seems like it should, but if it does it's too subtle for me to feel. I mean, among the sweetest rods I've ever owned or cast, some were hand planed and some (most, actually) were made on milling machines. I could sometimes tell the difference by looking at them very closely through a magnifying glass, but not by casting them. On the other hand, out of the six bamboo rods I've bought new in my life, five were hand planed, but the reasons for that aren't entirely practical.

(If I've been sounding cautious here, it's because I'd like to get through this without saying something I don't mean, but also without pissing off half the rod makers I know.)

Basically, what bamboo rod freaks admire are rods that cast well and that are beautifully made. They admire them enough that they'll snoop past a company name to find the craftsman responsible, and it doesn't seem to matter much whether his title is Master Rod Maker in Residence or Shop Foreman. Beyond that—and in ways that don't matter when you're out fishing—a rod you can call handmade is probably a little bit sexier.

There are actually more important things than how the splines are cut or how many people work in the shop, like the quality of the bamboo, for instance. The best bamboo for fly rods is aged, and the longer the better. You'll hear a lot of talk about pre-war or pre-embargo cane (that would be the Second World War and the cold war embargo of China) or about bamboo that's been aged for twenty years. You get the idea that bamboo is more like whiskey than like lumber.

Good bamboo is also dry, and the drier the better. Back to Garrison again: The story goes that he wouldn't build rods during the summer because he thought the humidity at his shop in upstate New York was too high. Maybe he went fishing instead.

Colorado has been a hotbed of bamboo rod making for quite a while, in part because of the semi-arid climate, although the good fly fishing doesn't hurt, either. The 1931 Granger catalog has a lot to say about the dry, high-altitude climate of

Denver: "This natural climatic advantage . . . gives the cane used for Granger rods a drying out and seasoning that could not be equaled by twenty years of natural seasoning in the ordinary climate."

More recently, Mike Clark spent a few years making rods in Arizona and, after he moved back to Colorado, he said the climate in the desert was even better than here, but there was a shortage of trout.

And then there's how the bamboo is treated. Some makers use it pretty much as it comes off the culm, and their rods are a pale straw color. It's a classic look and lots of great rods are made that way, but most makers temper the bamboo in ovens, or flame temper it with a torch, making it harder and turning it anywhere from a warm tan color to damned near chocolate brown. The bamboo on Granger rods was treated with ammonia steam that gave it a dark honey color. Sometimes the color is uniform, sometimes it's mottled, and the exact way the cane is flamed, baked, torched, tempered, or whatever can become part of a rod maker's signature.

Some rods are impregnated, that is, soaked in a solution that sinks right into the bamboo and then hardens to a finish that doesn't need varnish. Some of the old Wright & McGill Water Seal impregnated rods and Orvis Battenkills are a dark, dark brown, but I've seen impregnated rods that look like they were lightly flamed or baked. You can usually tell a darkly impregnated rod from a darkly flamed one, because with flaming the nodes will stand out as a light, golden tan.

Then there's node staggering: where you put the knots made by the nodes on the culm of bamboo as you arrange the splines on the rod itself. Nodes are both stiffer and weaker than the rest of the shaft, so where you put them can make some difference. There's the 3-3 system, opposing nodes, spiral nodes, and Garrison's elaborate pattern where no node is anywhere near another on the rod. It's sometimes called the Six Cylinder System because the nodes are staggered in the same order in which you'd time a six-cylinder engine.

Rod makers agonize about that, argue about it, and have been known to waste a lot of otherwise usable bamboo in order to get the node staggering the way they want it. A dealer once told me that any quality rod should have *some kind* of discernible node staggering, just to show that the guy gave it some thought, and that two nodes next to each other on adjacent splines means the rod is poorly made, period.

There's the density of the bamboo. Big, fat culms have bigger, stiffer fibers than small culms do. Use a culm of bamboo that's not suited to the taper you're making and you'll get a rod that's too stiff or one that doesn't have enough backbone. If you have a real understanding of your material, you'll choose the culm of bamboo that will work just right with the rod you're building. I've noticed that this can take considerable hefting, stroking, tapping, and staring out the window, so it may not be an entirely scientific process.

On the other hand, variations in the bamboo itself are why identical rods aren't always *exactly* identical. If you cast three rods of the same length, line weight, and model from the same maker, you may think one of them feels especially sweet, even though the other two aren't exactly dogs.

Some rod builders insist on making all the sections of a rod from the same culm of bamboo, placing the splines around the rod in the same order they came off the culm, and maybe even mirroring or book matching the tips so that all the nodes are in exactly the same place on both pieces. They say using the same cane throughout the rod makes for a more continuous, fluid action and that the matched tips will both flex in precisely the same way. As with hand planing versus milling, it *sounds* like it should make a difference.

The distance between nodes on the culm is also important: The more space between them, the better. The ideal culm would have no nodes at all, and naturally some makers over the years have tried scarfing the nodes out of their splines to make no-node or "sans node" rods. I've never cast one (there aren't that many around), but some people who have tell me the little bit of difference it makes probably isn't worth all the extra time and trouble on the part of the builder, let alone the expense if you want to buy one.

Water marks, cutter's marks, and other blemishes on the cane are usually just cosmetic, but most rod makers think the clarity of the bamboo is still important, if only for looks. A lot of buyers think that, too. (Cutter's marks are scratched signatures made by the workers who harvest the bamboo. Sometimes they're in really inconvenient places on the culm.)

Overall craftsmanship is pretty easy to recognize once you've looked closely at a few well-made rods. The glue joints between the splines should be tight and uniform with no lifts, gaps, or separations. If the maker used a clear glue, the joints will be invisible: It'll look like the flat sides of the blank were cut out of a single, straight-grained piece of material. If a dark glue was used, the glue line should be very thin and very uniform, like a fine pen line drawn against a ruler.

That kind of workmanship is its own reward, but I think there's also a practical reason for it. When a builder comes up with an especially sweet rod, he wants to be able to reproduce it, and the only way he can do that is by working to very fine tolerances. Rods that are put together sloppily can still work okay, but getting a good one is as chancy as picking the right whole-cane crappie pole from the barrel down at the hardware store.

A varnish finish on a rod should be smooth and even with no drips, trapped dust, or beard hairs. Other finishes, like tung oil or impregnation, should also be smooth and uniform.

The ferrules should be good-quality nickel silver and they should be set tight and flush with the rod shaft. The ferrule wraps that cover the spot where the ferrule and the cane come together should be smooth and even. The same goes for the guide wraps. The feet of the guides should be tapered with a file so the wraps run smoothly from the foot to the rod shaft.

Ferrules should fit together smoothly and tightly. They should pull apart smoothly, too, and make a nice, satisfying pop.

A new rod should be perfectly straight or have a slight curve upward—that is, away from the guides—and all the sections should be precisely the same length, although it's okay for the tip-top guides to extend the length of the wire loop above the rest of the sections. Some do, some don't.

Well, okay, sometimes you'll see a parabolic rod with a short butt and long tips, and Hardy made some rods with the tips sections intentionally ¼ to ½ inch shorter than the butts, but those are exceptions, and even then, both tips should be the same length.

And it should *have* two tips. Bamboo rods traditionally come that way.

Reel-seat hardware should be good quality and functional. At a bare minimum, it should fit your reel foot, hold the reel snugly, not work loose, and otherwise not be big and clunky. A lot of the modern rod makers use nickel-silver hardware on fancy wood spacers and that's almost become a standard. It's pretty, it's classy, and even a screw-locking seat doesn't add that much weight. On the other hand, lots and lots of classic rods used aluminum hardware and there's nothing wrong with it. There's nothing wrong with plain, straight-grained wood spacers, either.

Bamboo rods typically come in either two- or three-piece models. Customarily, most rods longer than 8 feet are in three pieces, two-piece rods are usually shorter than 8 feet, and an 8-footer itself can go either way, although there are plenty of exceptions to that. Some people prefer one design over another, but so many really fine classic rods were made in both configurations it's probably fair to say it doesn't matter. I guess I have a slight preference for three-piece rods because they're traditional and they're handy for traveling, but other than that I don't think it makes much difference.

Four-piece rods sound like they'd be handy for traveling, too, but they often have poor actions because there are too many ferrules, which usually makes them too stiff and tip heavy. Now and then you'll see a good one—I've heard the old Phillipson Smugglers were nice casting rods—but a lot of four-piece fly rods are lemons and you should probably be a little suspicious of them.

The rare rods with *more* than four pieces are probably not much more than curiosities. As someone once said, they amount to nickel-silver fly rods with split-bamboo trim.

One-piece rods are rare too, but you do see them now and then. Thomas & Thomas has made them, so have Robert Gorman, Mike Clark, and probably others I don't know about, almost always as custom orders. Fans of these things say a rod without a ferrule to interrupt the action is, as an old T&T catalog said, "The purest, most perfect" fly rod. The drawbacks are:

They're usually very expensive because they're so hard to make, there's naturally no such thing as a spare tip, and, as Mike once said, "Their portability sucks."

The overall style of a rod probably isn't that important as long as everything is neat and crisp, but the way a rod looks is really interesting because it reveals a lot about the maker.

I'll go back to Garrison again, because he's irresistible. His rods may or may not be the finest ever made, but they're sure the most understated. They were straight, amber-colored shafts with workmanlike cigar grips that tapered smoothly into cork or wooden reel seats with simple hooded caps and knurled-band hardware. The wraps were brown at the winding check and ferrules, and the guide wraps were white silk varnished without color preserver so they turned clear. The guides look like they're floating on the blank just under the varnish.

This guy was probably the most persnickety rod maker who ever lived, and his rods were absolutely plain and utilitarian.

Most of the Jim Payne rods have dark shafts, blued ferrules, quiet, earth-toned wraps, and dark wood reel-seat spacers with simple aluminum hardware. They look dignified and businesslike.

On the other hand, a Leonard Model 50, with its blond cane and bright red wraps, looks sort of bright and lively.

Grangers were wrapped differently depending on the model, and some of the wrap colors were more successful than others, but all except the early ones have that honey-colored bamboo, man-sized western-style grips, and the Granger all-metal up-locking or sliding-band reel seat. You can spot one across a crowded room.

The old, cheap rods usually *look* cheap, even if you can ignore the casual workmanship. A lot of them have tinny aluminum seats with Bakelite or plastic spacers, sometimes in unfortunate colors, but then that can be deceiving. Some really good rods—like the old Winstons—have Bakelite-and-aluminum reel seats, too, but the Bakelite is a formal black and the seats are better made and more gracefully designed. The reel seats on some of the cheap production rods look like something you'd find under the bathroom sink.

Most rod makers eventually settle on a certain look for their rods that they think makes them at least a little bit distinctive, but that's also handsome and traditional. Maybe it's a unique reel seat, a swelled butt, wrap colors, a signature wrap on the butt section, fine knurling on the hardware, a delicate little hook keeper built into a silver winding check, or whatever.

R. L. Winston rods and the beautiful rods made by Gary Howells, who once worked at Winston, are the only ones I've seen with the female ferrules wrapped entirely in thread. It looks sort of odd at first, but it's so much of a hallmark, and the rods by both makers are so consistently good, you eventually come to like it.

The standard F. E. Thomas signature wrap is three detached tags, then a space, then seven tags, another space, and then three more, with single, wider wraps framing it, one on the outside and one at the winding check, all in a dark burgundy-colored thread.

Mike Clark is one of those makers whose typical rod is hard to describe. He builds five more or less standard models (one with an elk antler reel-seat spacer), but most of his work is in custom rods, where the buyer decides on the reel-seat spacer, hardware, grip shape, wrap colors, and so on. Some of his rods are pale, blond cane; others are so darkly flamed you can hardly read the writing on the shaft. He's made more one-of-a-kind rods than any other rod builder I know. He says it keeps him from getting bored, but it's been said that in years to come collectors will hate him for it.

Some things you normally think of as purely cosmetic might actually make a difference. A proper varnish finish on a bamboo rod should leave the flat sides and corners of the blank distinct, not only because it looks neater, but also because too much varnish adds weight and muffles the action of the rod. Or at least that's what they say.

I like the looks of a swelled butt, but that fat part of the shaft just ahead of the cork grip stops the action, makes the grip rigid, and at least gives you the feeling of more leverage.

I prefer blued ferrules and reel-seat hardware because I think that's handsome, but there are those who say bright, polished hardware can flash in the sunlight and scare fish. I don't feel like I've ever spooked fish with bright hardware, but I have so many other ways of spooking them I guess I can use all the help I can get.

Typically, screw-locking reel seats with wood spacers are on longer, heavier rods that are intended to be worked hard, while cap-and-ring seats, sometimes with cork spacers, are on shorter, lighter rods to help *keep* them light.

Lately two rod makers I know have been burning up the phone lines looking for good-quality cork for their grips. (Rod makers hate the fact that the best stuff goes for the corks in wine bottles.) You could make a case that the easiest grip to hold onto with wet hands is one made of rougher, lower-quality cork rings, but smooth, uniform cork looks better to perfectionists, whether they're making the rods or buying them.

The shape of the cork grip can be part of a rod maker's signature and some of them are very distinctive, like the thumb-notch grips Wes Jordan liked, or the elliptical hammer-handle grips on some Grangers and Phillipsons. Some fishermen have real preferences about grip shapes, but for some reason I don't. The only grips I *don't* like are the little tiny handles on some of the small, light Leonards. They're just not big enough to get a hold of.

The type of ferrule you use is important, as is the guide spacing and the varnish and the glue. (Glue is the kind of thing that keeps rod makers awake at night, but that most fishermen don't even think about.) A whole bunch of other seemingly small things are important, too, but I'm beginning to get out of my depth here, into stuff I've been told but don't know enough to explain and about which different rod makers have different opinions anyway. I do know there can be hundreds of separate operations to making a bamboo fly rod and they all make some difference; some are so crucial and permanent that if you screw them up you have to dump the blank and start over from scratch. I also think that if the stuff you can see is done well, so is the stuff you *can't* see.

I have an old, nameless production rod that breaks all the rules. It's got cheap, nonwaterproof ferrules, a tin reel seat, and a cork grip shaped like a Polish sausage. The blank is lousy with lifts and gaps, there are two or three places on it where two nodes are right together, the cane itself is badly water marked, the varnish is so full of what looks like sawdust that it's rough to the touch, and it's wrapped in a hideous blue/yellow/red/green/orange-variegated thread. Oh yeah, and there's only one tip and none of the three sections are exactly the same length.

Oddly enough, it's not a half-bad 6-weight—not a sublime rod, but a passable day-to-day fishing pole—and it's beat up enough that it has clearly provided someone with a lifetime of hard fishing, which I can't quite turn up my nose at. It also has the added advantage that it cost twenty bucks at a yard sale, so if I slammed it in a car door tomorrow, or if it just fell apart on its own, I wouldn't have to shoot myself. A friend once told me it would make a good poacher's rod—you know, one you could ditch if the game warden showed up—although of course I have no use for such a thing.

That old clunker casts okay in spite of everything because it has a good taper—it's the only thing the maker did right, in fact. All things being equal, the taper is the heart and soul of a rod: the thing that makes it cast the way it's supposed to. Rod makers have always fooled around with their tapers and some great rod actions have been developed, but not many. If you start talking to rod makers and collectors, you begin to see that more than a century of experimentation has only turned up about twenty-five or thirty bamboo rod tapers that really work. They can be lengthened or shortened a little, tweaked a thousandth of an inch here or there to speed them up or slow them down, and they can sometimes be adjusted for different line weights, but that's about it.

Apparently, adjusting fly-rod tapers is in the same class with defusing bombs. I once listened to two rod makers talking about how you could add or subtract a thousandth of an inch in one place on a blank and it wouldn't make much difference, but if you did it somewhere else it would turn a good rod into either a worthless noodle or a crowbar.

I've also been told that just copying classic tapers isn't as foolproof as it sounds. Different bevelers and planing forms have their own subtle quirks, and even if you can get the taper exactly right, the quality and density of the bamboo, the way it's tempered, the glue you use, and all kinds of other mysterious things will affect the way the rod casts. In the end, even builders who work faithfully from time-honored tapers usually end up making rods that aren't precise copies of the originals.

My understanding is, if someone tells you they've come up with a completely new bamboo rod taper, chances are good they've either made a rod that doesn't work (which happens more often than you'd think) or they've accidentally rediscovered something.

Anyway, out of those twenty-five or thirty tapers, any normal, competent fly caster will like or appreciate or understand maybe half. That doesn't mean the other half aren't good, just that they're designed for different casting styles.

The difference between a bad taper and a good taper you just don't get is pretty hard to describe. I'll say that some of the Paul Young parabolic rods are sort of beyond me, probably because they're too demanding, but if I fool around with one long enough it will sooner or later show me how it's supposed to work, and it works gloriously. Trouble is, I want a rod that allows for a little more slop.

On the other hand, I can take a cheap-grade Bristol or Horrocks-Ibbotson down to the park, cast it all afternoon with several different fly lines, and never find the sweet spot, because there isn't one.

Another difference is, the low-grade Bristols and H-Is are generally considered to be not very good rods, while there's a good-sized cult of fishermen who think the Young parabolics have something to do with the meaning of life itself—and I'm not prepared to argue with them.

My friend Pat Leonard and I had a long talk about the quality of rods while sitting in a cafe in Wheatland, Wyoming, last fall. He said you can't say one rod is as good as another just because someone fishes it and likes it, because maybe that someone can't cast or has just never used a really good rod and so doesn't know the difference. Pat's in the music business, so his analogy was, the latest rap group is not necessarily in the same league with Charlie Parker just because they have some tin-eared fans. You have to allow for artistry and even genius.

Now, I don't make rods and, although I like to think I can recognize a good rod when I cast it, the actual tapers are sort of a mystery to me. Most of the rods I like are described as having "progressive" tapers, but among the others I like, a few are called "semiparabolics," never mind that a mathematician will tell you a curve is either parabolic or it's not. There's no such thing as a semiparabola.

Still, all I really know for sure is that most of these tapers were arrived at slowly by master craftsmen who were often working by the seat of their pants, or "empirically," as Ernest Schwiebert once put it. They're the result of time, tradition, thought, and trial and error.

There are some exceptions. Garrison was an engineer by trade and he worked out his tapers mathematically based on a series of stress tests. There are some people now doing the same kind of thing on computers—with mixed results.

Somehow we modern, technological humans have gotten two fallacies into our heads. One is that the current generation has to break completely with the old one in order to accomplish something new; the other is that doing something new is necessarily a good thing. In fact, the best work is still usually done in the oldest tradition of craftsmanship: You learn to do the thing the way it is: as the end product of generations of collective genius. That can amount to a life's work, and if you never get a new idea, fine. If you do get an idea, you'll probably have to try it. If it works you use it, if it doesn't you go back to the old ways and continue to do recognizably good work. Those who strike out on their own without first mastering the craft can end up on some pretty thin ice.

My own personal rule is: Beware of new tapers worked out on a computer. Computers don't fish and they don't even know what fishing is. Also: If the guy has to explain to you why the rod you're casting is a good one, it's not a good one for you.

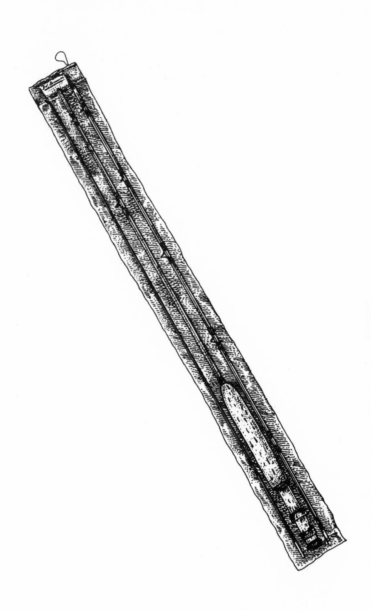

4

New Rods

OKAY, MAYBE IT'S finally time to talk about price. Bamboo fly rods, especially new ones, can go for what looks like a lot of money, and I know that scares off more people than it attracts. The people it *does* attract know that a lot of these rods hold their value and many of them appreciate over time, unlike new graphites, which, as A. K. once said, "are worth half what you paid for them the minute you drive them off the lot."

Bob Summers, the Traverse City, Michigan, rod maker, once told me about a guy who bought one of his rods new and then turned right around and sold it to a collector for more than he paid for it. I asked Bob if that pissed him off. He said, "I just raised my prices."

Still, I hesitate to call everyone who buys bamboo rods with an eye to their eventual increase in price an "investor," because many of these guys just aren't cold blooded enough. They fish

their rods and get to love them too much to ever sell them—
or they sell them only to buy other rods—so any profit they
realize is purely theoretical. Some even end up making philo-
sophical pronouncements like, "The price of some of these
things is just something you have to get past in order to appreciate their real value."

Over the last few years, I've seen rods by some new makers
who were competent but not yet well known going for $700 to
$800, and rods by established, famous makers with impressive
credentials going for as much as $1,600 or $1,700, with the
average price right around, say, $950 to $1,200.

To put that in a historical perspective, in 1912 my grandfather made $5 a week working sixty hours in a factory that
produced railroad cars, and that wasn't half bad. For instance, it
was enough to hire a woman to come in once a week and do the
laundry. As far as I know, my grandfather did not order a top-of-
the-line Orvis bamboo rod that year, but if he had, it would
have cost him $20: a month's pay at something like a normal,
blue-collar wage.

The same kind of job now pays maybe $12 an hour for more
like a forty-hour week, which comes to either $1,920 a month
or $2,880 for the same number of hours worked. A top-of-the-
line Orvis bamboo rod in the 1996 catalog goes for $1,450.
That's more expensive than most, but even at that it makes the
point: A fancy new bamboo fly rod is cheaper now than it was
in 1912, or, if you want to come at it from the other direction,
a good bamboo rod has *never* been cheap.

Of course, Grandpa wouldn't have ordered the top of the
line from Orvis or anyone else, if only because Grandma would
have tanned his hide for it. If he'd wanted a bamboo fly rod he'd
have gotten the one at the bottom of page twelve in the same

old Orvis catalog for $5 or, more likely, a perfectly usable rod from Sears for less than half that.

Those are the rods no one's making anymore: the ones that were pretty much replaced by fiberglass in the 1950s. Now there are still some real bargains in used bamboo rods—by bargains I mean they're very good, very usable rods that cost less than many new graphites—but as long as we're talking about new rods, let's go ahead and talk about them.

I know a small handful of individual bamboo rod makers and there's a larger handful I know *of*. All told, I think I've at least heard of most whose rods are more or less readily available, notwithstanding some pretty long waiting lists. Dealers and serious collectors tend to know of more rod makers who are either pretty new or pretty obscure, but even they get surprised periodically by good rods coming from some upstart they never heard of working out of his basement in Loose Gravel, Idaho.

I'm talking about professional rod makers, but I'm not exactly certain what I mean by professional. Someone with a brochure, stationery, and business cards; someone who sells, let's say, more than twenty rods a year; maybe someone who regularly sells rods to people he doesn't know personally, or who'll accept an order and sooner or later deliver the finished rod. Something like that, but not necessarily all of the above.

I'll take the gamble and list in the back of this book some of the professional bamboo rod makers I know of who are currently working and selling rods. If I mistakenly leave some out, all I can say is, I apologize and please send me a brochure in care of the publisher.

I don't want to be a stickler about who's a pro and who's not because I'm not qualified to judge anyone and it's probably none of my business anyway, but it's a distinction worth thinking about when you're shopping for a fly rod. It's true that some so-called amateurs—especially those who've gotten some honest advice from older makers and who are smart enough to work from traditional tapers—hit their stride early and end up making excellent, usable fly rods. Sometimes the most noticeable differences between their work and that of the big-name guys are price and panache—and maybe some fine points of cosmetics—and sometimes there are no differences at all. Not always, not even usually, but sometimes.

But then it's also true that rod makers who can claim apostolic succession going back several generations and/or who have been making rods full time for quite a few years and have respectable reputations are more likely to make really fine rods than hobbyists or craftsmen who are just starting out. Mike once told me that even now, after over fifteen years of building and selling rods, he thinks he learns an average of one new, usable thing on every second or third rod he makes, and the more rods you can multiply that by, the more skill you're looking at.

In the long run, fine craftsmanship comes from endless, laborious, intelligent repetition, so the people who've been at it the longest are usually the best. The refinements in their rods can be obvious or subtle—sometimes it comes down to something as vague as a certain heft or feel—but if the rod costs you a little more, you're usually paying for more than just glitz and a recognizable name.

But will you actually cast better or catch more fish with a $1,400 rod than with a $900 one? Nine times out of ten, yes.

I also have to say that most new rods by modern makers are definitely worth what they cost, if only because of the realities of life. If you add up the hours it takes a craftsman to make a rod and then subtract the overhead (material, rent or mortgage, tools and equipment), you're looking at a self-employed artisan with rare skills and years of experience pulling down less than he could make putting widgets on gizmos in a factory. Whatever the actual value of something like a bamboo fly rod, it ought to sell for at least enough for the guy who built it to make a living.

A lot of bamboo fishermen and collectors still consider the Orvis, Thomas & Thomas, and R. L. Winston Companies to be production rod makers, and I guess they are in the sense that the rods bear company names and the shops are parts of larger operations that between them sell everything from graphite rods to mailboxes with leaping trout on them.

Be that as it may, these bamboo rod shops amount to enclaves with a handful of employees doing fine work, and in that sense they're a lot more like the great old shops of Payne and Thomas than they are like, say, Montague or South Bend, let alone some corporate monolith.

I'm not that familiar with the recent Orvis rods, but I can say that the Winstons and the T&Ts are typically as good as any of the handmade rods and, give or take a few bucks one way or the other, they're comparably priced. The main difference is, the companies produce more rods than the lonesome craftsmen, so you usually don't have to wait as long to get one.

(Then again, waiting a year or more for someone to make you the rod you want is an interesting exercise for those of us who've gotten used to instant gratification. It might even do us some good.)

Some collectors and dealers say the rods by these companies don't hold their value as well or appreciate as quickly as the good handmade rods. That's more or less true, but it's also sort of a fine point. Used T&T and Winston rods are far from cheap, and, although many Orvis rods are bargains used, you have to remember that there are a hell of a lot of them out there. Orvis has been in business since before the Civil War, and since then there have been a lot of rods made, some of which were intentionally inexpensive, and over the years there's been some variation in quality.

And anyway, I don't recommend buying bamboo rods in order to turn a profit. I recommend buying rods you want to fish. I've talked to several rod makers who've sold new rods to people who immediately put them under glass as works of art or, worse yet, stashed them in dark closets as investments. The makers all had more or less the same take on that: They were mildly flattered and more than a little bit annoyed. As one man said, "People like my rods because they *cast well*, goddamn it!"

I suppose an exception to that would be something like the beautiful and expensive Thomas & Thomas limited-edition rods and some of Walt Carpenter's snazzier models that were made to be collector's items. That kind of thing goes on and there's nothing wrong with it, but when I say "fly rods," I mean *fishing* rods.

In his book *The Sporting Craftsmen*, Art Carter wrote about good new bamboo fly rods by companies and individual makers pretty much in the same breath, and I think that was wise and perceptive. In the long run, it's the quality of the rod that counts, and in the *really* long run, the next generation of dealers and collectors will have plenty of time to sort it out.

I usually learn about new, independent makers through conversations with other bamboo rod nuts, by reading about their rods in dealers' rod lists, and sometimes by just stumbling across them. I don't know how many times I've gone someplace to fish—someplace with a town nearby, that is—and heard about a bamboo rod maker living in the area or even seen one of his rods at the local fly shop, usually for sale on consignment.

By "new maker" I mean new to me. Some of these people turn out to have been working with bamboo rods for decades, but at such a low volume that you just don't hear about them outside of their home counties. These guys always interest me because you don't make rods for twenty years without learning something.

There's no standard profile of a bamboo rod maker (except that after a certain number of years they all seem to get a little cranky and opinionated), but it's surprising how many of them are those all-around handy types. You know, people who spent their childhoods disassembling clocks and toasters and their teenage weekends rebuilding cars under shade trees in the back-yard. Many of them were trained as engineers and/or machinists, although they could just as well be anything from jewelers to musicians to heavy-equipment operators. Whatever, they're of that breed that isn't satisfied that something works; they've gotta know how and why.

It's been interesting watching Mike Clark over the last fif-teen years or so. The rods he makes now are really fine—they cast beautifully, they're pretty as hell, and I say that only partly as a friend—but I don't think he'll mind me saying that his early rods were not especially pretty. He didn't worry about that at first. He started out trying to make rods that cast well, and I remember seeing the same cheap, green-anodized reel seat on several successive rods, sometimes with the guides taped on with duct tape so he could fool around with the spacing. When a rod didn't cast right, as a lot of the early ones didn't, he'd sal-vage the valuable hardware to use on the next prototype, and the blank would go in the woodstove. Once he got them to cast right, he started worrying about how they looked.

I've heard it said that some of the new rod makers just coming up are doing it backward: They're making rods that are pretty enough but don't cast well. To be a successful bamboo rod maker, though, you eventually have to work out both the performance *and* the looks—and it's a craft that takes years to master—so maybe it doesn't matter where you start. On the other hand, if it was my rod, I'd rather have people say, "Well, it's not the prettiest thing I ever saw, but it sure casts nice."

Some rod makers are a lot like artists or writers: They start small, working part time, then get the hang of it and begin to gain a local reputation. Sometimes it stops there, and that's not necessarily bad. After all, turning something you love into a business isn't always the smartest thing you could do, and it's possible to find happiness making your own rods and maybe selling just enough to friends to cover the cost of your tools and material or pay for a nice fishing trip now and then.

Even among the big-name makers, the business is still mostly word of mouth. Now and then you'll see a story. *The New Yorker* once did a long article on Ron Kusse, *Fortune Magazine* included Walt Carpenter's rods in a thing called "100 Products America Makes Best," and so on. The magazine sections of local newspapers like rod makers because they seem quaint, which is always a nice, safe weekend-supplement angle. Nine times out of ten, the reporters know very little about fishing, let alone fly rods, and they portray the rod maker as the last stubborn holdout in a dying art form. A young reporter interviewing a rod builder with any gray at all in his hair will invariably refer to him as The Old Master. If the makers aren't embarrassed by that, they should be.

Sometimes you'll see small black-and-white ads in the fly-fishing magazines for bamboo rod makers, but many of the biggest names are absent. It's true that some of these guys are back-ordered for a year or more with new orders trickling in more or less on their own, so they don't *have* to advertise. Different rod makers give different estimates on how long it takes to make a rod, but if you can come in under forty hours (not counting several drying sessions for glues and varnish coats) you're doing well, and if you turn out forty or fifty rods a year working alone, I don't know when you have time to either sleep or go fishing.

Another problem is, it's hard to figure out *where* to advertise (magazine ad-department demographics usually don't mention bamboo rods), and, after all, individual rod makers are working artisans who often don't have much of an advertising budget anyway.

So the standard vehicle is the brochure, which can be sort of a circular affair. You get a brochure by writing to the maker and asking for one, but in some cases the only way to get his address is from the brochure.

Brochures are interesting and sometimes they're deeply revealing of the character of the rod maker, but I've never seen one that told me what I really wanted to know. Namely, will one of these rods ring my chimes or not? The only way you'll even get a hint at that is by casting the rod on the grass, and the only way you'll know for sure is by fishing it for a few weeks. For reasons I'll probably never understand, I've had a few rods that cast beautifully down at the park, and that worked pretty well on the water, too, but that somehow just never quite got it in the long run.

Still, since you might not be able to travel the country trying out fly rods, you can end up buying one blind: on faith, reputation, and advice from friends. I've heard of makers ship-ping rods to customers to try out, but you can't count on that. Sometimes there isn't a finished rod on hand that isn't already spoken for, and even if there is, this is a service that's often reserved for friends and old regular customers.

And before you write that off as arrogance, ask yourself if you'd send $1,000 fly rods to one total stranger after another.

Now that I think about it, I've never bought a new rod from a maker I didn't know personally, but it's surprising to me how many people are perfectly satisfied with rods they've bought sight unseen. Maybe it's because they've done a lot of snooping around, maybe even cast some of the maker's other rods, or at least talked to some people who own them. Or maybe it's because the maker himself has interrogated the guy pretty thor-oughly, trying to find out what kind of fishing he does, what other rods he likes, and such.

Also, most rod builders eventually become known for mak-ing a certain kind of rod, so if you like a quick, progressive dry-fly action, you won't seek out someone who's famous for his laid-back parabolics.

Ed has a good trick. He says he asks every maker he meets which rod best exemplifies his own particular style of rod making. So far, he tells me, every maker he's talked to has known exactly which rod to pick up.

Of course, there are customers from hell. A well-known maker I know sold a rod to a man not long ago, and it was an unusual case because the customer actually went to the shop, cast the rod, and liked it. But then a week or so later he came back wanting to return it. He said, "This rod breaks off fish," which is sort of like bringing a car back to the lot and saying, "This thing runs into telephone poles."

I cast that rod myself and, sure enough, if you were fishing a 7X tippet and struck too hard, you could break a fish off with it. The new owner loves it, fishes it every chance he gets, and he was delighted to get bumped ahead on the waiting list.

If you get into bamboo rods, you'll probably become insatiably curious about them. There are books that'll tell you how they're made and who's made them over the years, but the only way to really learn about them as a fisherman is to fish with them. There are only a handful of real bamboo rod experts around and most of them are either dealers who've seen thousands of rods, longtime makers who've built and restored hundreds, or serious (that is, wealthy) collectors. I know a man who owns, at last count, something like fifty bamboo rods. I once asked him, "Why so many?" He said, "I wanted to learn about them."

In fact, most of the bamboo fishermen I know have gone through some rods to find the ones they like to fish with and will never sell—sometimes a handful, sometimes dozens. That's why there's a used-rod market, and rods by contemporary makers do show up there now and then. On the other hand, I know some people who keep threatening to sell off all but the three or four rods they fish regularly, but who never quite get around to doing it.

Wanting to cast—if not actually own—every rod by every maker is like wanting to fish every trout stream in North America: You'll probably never do it, but it might be worth a try. On the other hand, you can't buy every good rod that comes along. I mean, even if you could afford it, what would you do with them? That guy I know with fifty rods hasn't even cast them all, let alone fished them.

When it comes right down to it, most of us want more rods than we have, even though we probably already have too many and would be much better casters if we stuck to that handful of old favorites.

Anyway, the more different rods you cast, the more you'll learn and the more informed your tastes will become, but even those who have a lot of experience with new rods eventually end up developing a relationship with a couple of makers whose work they admire, whose rods fit their own particular casting style, and, often enough, whom they just like as friends.

And anyway, tying out too many rods can be dangerous.

Early last September, I'd have told you I had all the 7½-foot rods I needed. There's an old Thomas & Thomas Special Trouter, an even older F. E. Thomas Special, a sweet H. L. Leonard 39DF, a G. E. Lipp Impregnated (one of only about twenty ever made), and an F. D. Lyons three-piece built from blanks he said he thought came from the old F. E. Thomas shop.

But then John Bradford came through town on his way back to Texas after a fishing trip in Wyoming. Naturally, he had some of his rods with him, and naturally, we had to go down to the park to try them out.

He handed me a 7½-foot 5-weight and said, "I think you might appreciate this." I took that to mean he thought better of my casting than he once had. Years ago, as I was stringing up one of John's rods to try out on a casting pool, he said, "That's a real gentleman's rod; you probably won't like it."

Naturally, I bought the rod. (I guess I'm just a sucker for the soft sales pitch.) Also, when I went home that day, there was a check waiting for me in the mailbox the amount of which made me think I was *meant* to own that rod. Freelance writers live from check to check anyway, and we've been known to attach mystical significance to things like that.

I have to say I bought that rod partly for sentimental reasons. By that I mean, it's a beautifully made rod that looks great and casts wonderfully, but it was also built by a man I know and like, and it's more than just poetic mush to say that something of the maker is *in* the rod.

By "something" I mean something good, probably even the best the guy has to offer. Someone once said of a slightly short-tempered rod maker we both know, "If his *entire* personality was in these rods, they'd all be 12-weights."

The next morning John left for Texas and Mike, A. K., Ed, and I went over to the Frying Pan River to fish for a week. (I figured I'd better get the hell out of town before another rod maker showed up.) I took the 7½-foot Bradford and fished it hard. A gleaming new bamboo rod is sort of intimidating and I've found the best thing to do with one is to immediately suck it up, catch as many fish as you can on it, and at least get the cork grip dirty.

When I got home I wrote to Bradford. I said I figured I'd started catching fish on his rod before he'd made it to the New Mexico border.

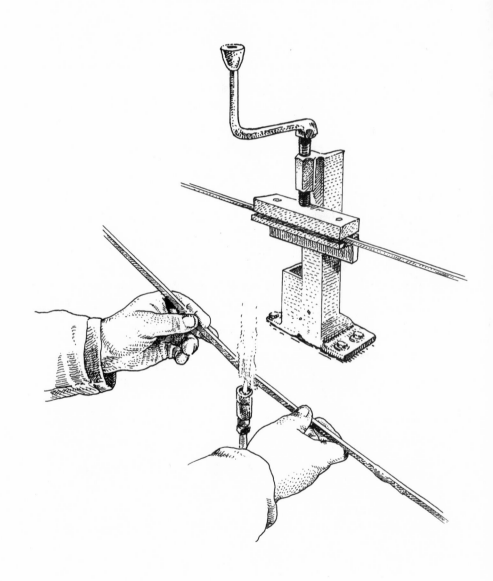

5

Old Rods

I DO HAVE MORE bamboo fly rods than I really need, but I don't consider myself a collector. My only defense is, although I have a few rods I don't fish and a few others I rarely fish, I never bought one I didn't *intend* to fish. I'm also lucky enough not to have the collector's manias for completeness and perfection. I don't feel the need to own, say, every model of rod the Heddon Company ever made—in mint, unfished condition.

Almost all the bamboo fly rods I've ever had have been used in the truest sense—that is, previously fished as well as previously owned—because those were the ones I could afford. At the same time, I guess I've developed a collector's sensibilities out of self-defense. I've always been a bargain hunter by necessity, and finding good rods that don't cost a fortune is like locating good fishing spots by not going where everyone else goes.

Good old bamboo fly rods do still turn up at yard sales, flea markets, and auctions, although not as often as they used to.

There was a time when you could almost count on sooner or later picking up a bargain in a place like that—say, a serviceable Heddon or Phillipson for $25—but now that people have gotten it into their heads that all bamboo rods are fabulous collector's items, you're more likely to find a broken Montague with a $1,000 price tag on it. The same goes for antiques shops and about 90 percent of the joints that say "ANTIQUES & JUNQUE."

Sometimes you'll see good old rods for sale in the classified ads, sometimes they turn up at fly shops—again, not as often as they used to—and if you become known in local fishing circles as one of those weird guys who fish with bamboo fly rods, you might even get a phone call from someone wanting to sell one. I got a wonderful Granger Favorite when a man in his late seventies called and said he wanted to sell his old fly rod to someone who'd use it. I told him he'd reached the right guy.

And yes, it *was* a little sad that he couldn't fish it himself anymore. On the other hand, meeting the man and hearing some of his stories somehow added some karma to that rod. Maybe that's why I almost always catch fish with it.

But really, the best way to find old bamboo fly rods is through people who deal in them, either professionally or casually. I know of five more or less official catalogs of used rods, reels, and other fishing related stuff: There's Len Codella's *Heritage Sporting Collectibles*, Bob Corsetti's *Rods & Reels*, Martin Keane's *Classic Rods & Tackle*, Carmine Lisella's *Jordan-Mills Rod Co.*, and Dick Spurr's *The Classic Chronicle*.

By "official" I mean they're bound, usually illustrated, and arrive more or less regularly, which doesn't necessarily mean they always have the best rods or the best prices. There are at least that many more stapled, photocopied lists that come out more or less regularly.

Other lists come out irregularly—like the great one Tom Clark issues from Michigan now and then—or maybe even just once, when a collector wants to move some rods or a builder ends up with too many good used rods cluttering up his shop. Walt Carpenter sends out a list occasionally. It's usually short and the stuff is usually very good.

I continue to learn about these things by looking in the classified ads in fly-fishing magazines and by talking to friends, collectors, and dealers I know. (Like rod builders, some of the biggest dealers don't advertise because they don't have to.) I get every list I can find, but I suspect there are a few floating around out there that I don't know about, and that worries me deeply.

Anyway, if you read these lists long enough you'll see it all, from the sublime to the pure crap. Eventually you'll begin to get a feel for what old rods are worth and why.

In the grand scheme of things, I suppose museum-piece rods with true historical significance are worth as much as anyone is willing to pay for them, which is apparently a hell of a lot. Exactly which rods those are can make for an interesting argument, but it's not an argument I've ever taken part in. The most expensive rod I've so far seen for sale was being offered at $10,000. I think it was a Gillum, although it could just as easily have been a Garrison. The price freaked me out so much I forgot who made the rod.

It wasn't in the next list, so I assume someone bought it and I remember wondering what the hell the guy was thinking. That's about the extent of my interest in the really big-ticket stuff.

At the other end are the cheap mass-produced rods by companies like Montague, Bristol, Horrocks-Ibbotson, Shakespeare, and South Bend, plus many of the hardware store or trade rods that were made by production companies and sold under names like Abbey & Imbrie, J. C. Higgins, Union Hardware, Spaulding, Lyon & Coulson, Weber, Montgomery-Ward, and lots of others. This is a huge category and it includes many of the rods that aren't worth buying or fishing, although naturally there are some exceptions.

The collectible-rod market is a weird one in that the true antiques aren't the really hot items. The gems are the rods from the Golden Age, from the 1930s to the 1960s, because that's when fly rods became recognizably modern in their lengths and actions. Antique rods are typically long, heavy, sometimes ornate, always interesting, and, unless they were made by Hiram Leonard himself or were once owned by a famous dead fly-fishing writer, they're also pretty cheap.

The usable, affordable bamboo fly rods are in the middle somewhere—and the middle has a way of shifting around.

The prices of used bamboo fly rods have been going up ever since I've been watching them, and they'll probably continue to do that. Some of it has amounted to a normal cost of living increase, but prices are driven more by collectors than by fishermen, so there are some stranger things going on, too.

For instance, many of the Leonard rods were pretty seriously collectible even before the company finally closed its doors in the early 1980s, but sometime in the late 1980s something happened with the availability of the best Leonards and what one dealer described to me as "an influx of new collectors in the market," and the prices of some of the sexier models lurched upward. As you'd expect, when something like that happens a number of rods come out of the closet and onto the market.

(By the way, in 1995 Brian McGrath resurrected the old H. L. Leonard Rod Company. They're turning out twenty bamboo fly rods a year designed by none other than Tom Maxwell himself.)

The old Fred Divine rods had always been pretty inexpensive, but after rod historian Michael Sinclair published his book *Fishing Rods by Divine* in 1993, the prices of the better Divine rods bumped up a little. Not a lot, but enough to notice.

F. E. Thomas rods used to be fairly reasonable, but then some of the top rods by makers like Jim Payne began to get so valuable that Payne rods in the less desirable lengths and line weights went up in price just because of the name, and the Thomas rods sort of filled the vacuum they left behind.

Similar things have happened with other rods. For instance, I knew something was up when the catalog listings started changing from "old Granger" to "*historic, early* Granger."

Still, through all that, the rods I feel comfortable about buying (as opposed to the ones I feel *un*comfortable about, but still sometimes buy anyway) have stayed about the same: Grangers, Phillipsons, better-model Heddons, some of the workhorse Orvis rods like the impregnated Battenkills, the better-grade trade rods, and some of the less desirable models by some otherwise fairly high-ticket makers.

Now you have to understand that what collectors mean by "desirable" and "undesirable" models doesn't necessarily have anything to do with how useful they are as fishing rods. In fact, sometimes it's just the opposite. The most expensive rod from any collectible maker or company is usually the short, light one, so, all things being equal, a 9-foot 6-weight will cost roughly a third the price of a 7½-foot 4-weight by the same maker, even though the 7½-footer isn't the most versatile rod.

It's mostly a matter of scarcity. A lot of the modern makers specialize in delicate little rods, and some don't make anything beefier than a 7½- or 8-foot 5-weight, but for the better part of this century the standard bamboo trout rod was more like 8½ or 9 feet.

That makes sense, especially here in the West. On a normal knock-around day of fishing where you aren't sure if you'll end up on a stream or a lake, where you could go from casting dry flies to chucking streamers in the wind, and where you might even hang a good-sized fish, something like a 9-foot 6-weight is the rod that'll get you through.

If you ask a collector why a 7½-foot rod is so much more valuable, he'll say it's because it's real nice and it's rare. I always like to ask, "If it's so nice, how come it *is* so rare?—I mean, why did these guys make so many more 8½- and 9-foot rods than they did 7½-footers?"

I do have some 7½-foot, 4- and 5-weight rods—plus a 7-foot, 9-incher. I use them a lot on small mountain streams and medium-sized creeks and love them dearly, but I think anything shorter and lighter than that is too specialized to be very useful. If you're spooking fish with an 8-foot, 5-weight rod, the answer probably isn't a 7-foot 3-weight. The answer is a longer leader and a better cast.

I do have a little 3-weight that I ended up with after one of those elaborate trades you can get into, but I hardly ever use it. It's nice for little brook trout in beaver ponds as long as the wind doesn't blow, and it's fun on bluegills, but it won't cast a #12 popper. I think of it as a toy, although I've been told that if I lived back East where the wind never blows and the trout are all little, I'd take it more seriously.

I also suspect that ultralight rods—especially bamboo rods, which people tend to be very careful with—can kill fish. I like a rod with the backbone to play and land a decent-sized fish before he's been played to death.

Those short, light little rods have also given bamboo its reputation for not being powerful, but of course they weren't meant to be. You want power, try an 8-foot, 8-weight Orvis Wes Jordan or an 8½-foot, 7-weight Winston.

A lot of people who get that first bamboo rod end up with an ultralight little wand for special occasions, and I think that's a mistake. It's a rod you probably won't fish very often and if you get it thinking a light rod will make little fish seem big, you'll be disappointed. As a friend said the other day, "A 6-inch brook trout is a 6-inch brook trout, whatever you catch it on."

If you want to fish with a bamboo rod, get one you'll fish with: something like an 8½-foot 5-weight.

I guess my favorite all-around fly rod is my 8½-foot, 5-weight Mike Clark, followed closely by a couple of Grangers and a Phillipson in the same length and weight, a 9-foot, 6-weight Wright & McGill Granger Victory, a 9-foot, 5-weight Jim Payne 208 Light Dry Fly rod, and an 8-foot, 5-weight R. L. Winston. They're not exactly thunder sticks—in fact, they're all capable of surprising delicacy—but they've also got enough juice to throw long casts, deal with some wind, and play good-sized fish with some authority. A rod I've been sort of idly shopping for— and that I can probably afford—is one of the old Granger Model 9050s, which is another 9-foot 5-weight. I have a real soft spot for the 9-footers because they're damned efficient fly rods, they're what the regular old fisherman used to use, and, as I said, they're relatively cheap.

Well, okay, the Paynes and some other big-name 9-footers are sort of creeping up there now, but you can still find perfectly fishable 9-foot Grangers, Phillipsons, Heddons, and others—at this writing, in the winter of 1996–97—for not much over $200, and many of the 8½-footers are still around $300 or so. Those prices will change with time—everything does—but I suspect they'll stay the same relative to the cost of a new, top-of-the-line graphite, which can now go for $500 or more.

By the way, is it just my imagination, or is the standard graphite rod also 9 feet long?

Aside from the few new rods I've gotten my hands on—and that I'm damned happy to have—most of my rods were bought pretty cheaply, some long enough ago that they were just barely out of the decent-old-fishing-pole category. A few of those have now appreciated into collectible status and are worth considerably more than I paid for them.

I have mixed feelings about that. It's fun to own a couple of rods you couldn't afford to buy now, but, *because* you couldn't afford them now, you can get a little spooky about fishing them. I'm careful enough with my rods (no one wants to break a favorite rod, regardless of how much or how little it's supposedly worth) but I don't like to be paranoid and I don't like to let myself be intimidated by money.

So far this hasn't been a huge problem for me, but I've seen other fishermen agonize greatly about it. My friend Pat Leonard has a thing for Leonard rods. (He says the coincidence with the names is just that, a coincidence, but I told him he's still lucky his name isn't Pat Garrison.) Anyway, he has some fine old Leonards and he fishes them casually, but then he recently bought a beautiful 7-foot, 4-weight Jim Payne rod in mint, unfished condition. I guess what he paid for it is no one's business, but it was a lot, and last summer he asked me if I thought he should fish it or just look at it.

I said I didn't know; that I'd never buy a rod I was afraid to fish and if I somehow ended up with one (say, I found a museum piece at a yard sale for $5) I think I'd sell it and buy a dozen rods I *could* fish.

I've heard people say rods like this are collector's items in the best sense: There aren't that many of them, there will never be any more, and the few left in new condition should probably be preserved, both for posterity and to show proper reverence for the craftsmen who made them.

I've heard others say the way to show proper reverence for a rod like this is to do what the late Mr. Payne intended and go catch some fish on the damned thing. People with unfished rods under glass remind me of some book collectors I've met with pristine first editions and then some junky old paperback "reader's copies," as if reading a book amounted to abusing it.

Better to sidestep the problem altogether by not buying rods that terrify you.

All kinds of things come together to determine the value of a used rod. There's the maker, of course, and anyone who shops for old bamboo fly rods will begin to pick up a little history just by reading the descriptions of rods in the catalogs. A fair rule of thumb is, the longer the description, the more legendary the maker and the higher the price. Three-fourths of the rods I've bought came in at under four sentences.

As I said before, there's length and line weight, and it's almost always true that the longer a rod is and the heavier the line it carries, the cheaper it is compared to the shorter, lighter rods by the same maker. With a few exceptions, if you're looking for a bass, big trout, or salmon rod 9 feet or longer for a 6-, 7-, or 8-weight line, you're shopping in the discount store.

There can be some interesting juxtapositions here. A rare 7½-foot, 5-weight Montague might be worth about the same as a 9-foot Granger. A 7½-foot Granger in one of the snazzier grades can cost you roughly the same as a 9-foot Payne. A 7½-foot Payne could run you about the same as, say, a 9-foot Gillum in less than mint condition. And so on.

The condition of a rod is crucial to its value, and condition can be pretty subjective. You'll see rods described anywhere from "mint, unfished" to "near mint," "new," "near new," "excellent," "very good," "good," "solid," and "fishable as is," and also "restored" or "refinished" (sometimes "*professionally* refinished"), some combination like "mint-restored," sometimes followed by a plus or minus (as in "good +") or something like "excellent-refinished (exception noted.)" The exception could be as inconsequential as a replacement wrap or a stripping guide that isn't original, or something as serious as two broken tips.

There's a lot of leeway in there, but you'll notice it all sounds promising.

"What kind of shape is the rod in?"

"Well, it's good. It's fishable as is."

Some dealers are more charitable than others when it comes to condition and each one has his own idiosyncrasies. Marty Keane, for instance, is famous for the poetry and enthusiasm of his rod descriptions. The only category everyone agrees on completely is "mint, unfished," but in general the descriptions of the rods in most lists are more honest than, say, a real estate ad describing some old ruin of a house as "charming."

Still, you have to read catalog listings carefully and critically, and then meticulously inspect any rod you order, keeping in mind that something a collector would say injures the authenticity of a rod might either make no difference to you or maybe even improve the thing slightly.

I have an old 8½-foot, 7-weight Orvis Battenkill that's completely original except that I had the tiny little stripping guide replaced with a larger one. It's the same style of red agate guide and the new wraps are a good match for the old ones, but an Orvis nut would turn his nose up at it and a dealer who noticed the change would knock a few bucks off the price because of it.

Of course, all it means to me is that I can shoot a few more feet of line.

Because condition can be sort of a judgment call, not to mention descriptions of how a rod casts, just about all dealers offer a three-day inspection/return privilege, and it's entirely okay to call and ask about the rod in more detail. Some dealers even encourage you to do that, and if you see a rod you want, you'd *better* call, because if you don't someone else will. I've called on rods within minutes of getting the list out of the mailbox, and they'd already been sold.

The point is, anything that's wrong with a rod should lower the price, even if it doesn't lower its value as a fishing rod. Most of my old rods were described as being in "fishable as is" to maybe "very good" condition, which meant they showed signs of honorable use. I don't mind that a bit. In fact, I prefer it. As long as the rod is all there, the ferrules are tight, the finish is more or less intact, and the wraps are good, I'm happy. If it's a little beat up (as opposed to abused or broken), fine. I was gonna beat it up myself anyway.

Rods with broken and repaired sections (they're usually the tips) can be real bargains, but on a case-by-case basis. I can get as mystical about tapers as the next guy and I'm not entirely thrilled with broken rods, but I've cast a surprising number of bamboo rods that had one or both tips down an inch or so and it didn't seem to make any difference at all. I have a neat old F. E. Thomas Special like that. It's a 7½-foot, 2-piece 5-weight with one tip down an inch and, honestly, I can't tell the difference between the good tip and the short one. Otherwise the thing was in great shape when I bought it except the reel-seat spacer showed marks from a reel foot, the varnish was less than perfect, and the cork grip was dirty. Big deal.

As a general rule, a rod with one or both tips down, say, not much more than an inch stands a fair chance of being okay, but a tip missing 3 or 4 inches will probably be useless.

You see this kind of thing all the time: Four or five little flaws conspire to lower the price of a rod that would be pretty steep in mint condition. It's all there and in really nice shape except one tip is down an inch, some of the bluing is worn off the reel-seat hardware, there are a few bag marks in the varnish on the butt section, two of the guides are replacements and the wrap colors don't match exactly (although that's hard to see if you're not looking for it), it's not in the original bag, and the label is missing from the rod tube. Most rod descriptions are just that meticulous, which gives you a sense of how anal retentive some collectors are.

A rod in mint-restored or -refinished condition should be worth less than the same one in mint *original* condition, but more than if it was in, say, "good" shape.

The name of a previous owner written on the butt section is another thing that should knock a few dollars off the price of a rod—unless the previous owner was Lee Wulff, in which case it'll double it.

Repair wraps anywhere on the rod reduce its value and they're always a gamble. The standard repair wrap is tightly wound white silk varnished without color preserver so it's clear. If it's done well, it'll be a smooth, slightly raised spot on the shaft. Sometimes they're so neatly done you have to feel for them with your fingers. The problem is, you don't know what's under there. Maybe just a little hook ding, maybe six splintered splines. A good rule of thumb is, the longer the repair wrap, the more suspicious you should be.

A replacement tip by the original maker will lower the price less than a replacement tip of the same quality from someone else, while a missing tip on a two-tip rod should knock the price way down.

I have an old 8½-foot, 8-weight Leonard Tournament with three tips. Two are originals, one of which is the full length but with a repair wrap, and the third is a later replacement tip from the Leonard factory. It's a good model from a good maker and a great bass and pike rod but, because of the length, the line weight, and the weirdness with the tips, I don't have much in it.

Repaired rods are one thing, but rods that *need* repairs are another. I've known people who've done minor repairs on their rods and had pretty good luck. But then I've also heard horror stories about ham-handed klutzes who've reduced fine old fly rods to kindling wood. I think home bamboo rod repair is in a class with home gunsmithing, the only difference being, if you screw up a rod, it's unlikely to blow your hand off.

It's hard to find people who can do quality repairs on bamboo rods, let alone full restorations. Most of them are rod builders, their work isn't cheap, they'd really rather be making their own rods than fixing yours, there can be a pretty long wait involved, and, when it's all said and done, it's possible to end up with more money in a restoration job than the rod itself is worth. That's why it's not as arrogant as it sounds when some-one says, "I won't work on just any old rod."

I don't work on my own rods past putting some fresh spar varnish on dried-out wraps and minor hook dings, rewrapping a guide, or washing several decades worth of sweat and fly flotant off a cork grip. I also don't buy rods that *need* work until I find out what it'll cost and about how long it'll take.

I also try not to be too eager to have a rod refinished. If it has loose ferrules I'll have them fixed, and if the finish is bad enough to let water into the cane I'll have it redipped. But if it just has sun-faded wraps, age-darkened varnish, worn bluing, and a sweat-stained grip, I'll usually leave it alone. An old, well-used rod usually has some dignity and character to it, and sometimes an old refinished rod can come off like a middle-aged dude with gold chains and a hairpiece.

A lot of the old makers offered rods in different grades at different, sometimes *vastly* different, prices. Sometimes the grade indicated a difference in the quality of the rod and some-times it didn't, at least not in any way you'll care about while you're fishing it.

In 1941 Granger had the Registered selling for $75, the Premier for $50, the De Luxe for $37.50, the Favorite for $30, the Aristocrat for $25, the Special for $20, the Victory for $15, and the Champion for $12. Those rods were all virtually identical, with the same mildly swelled butts, the same hardware and reel seats, and the same actions. The only real differences were the clarity of the cane and the wrap colors. Still, a used Premier or De Luxe will cost you more than a comparable Champion—or maybe a Stream and Lake, another one of their low-end models.

A Granger Registered—if you ever see one—will be way too expensive because so few were made. Best to leave them for the serious collectors.

And then rods actually made by the Granger Company usually go for a little more than the ones made by Wright & McGill under the Granger name, even though the Wright & McGill Grangers were made in the same factory on the same machines by many of the same people. On the other hand, early Grangers—those with full-metal, sliding-band reel seats— are said to be inferior to the later ones with the locking seats. I don't agree with that, but it's what some collectors say, and they're the ones who set the prices.

Phillipsons are the same way. When they were new, the prices varied quite a bit—in 1947 the Premium sold for $75, the bottom-end Pacemaker for $25, with the Powr Pakt and the Paramount in between—but in terms of their quality as fishing rods, there wasn't much difference among them. Phillipsons varied a lot in appearance over the years and, since they were made in this part of the country, there are still plenty around. I've seen some that were fairly unattractive, but I've never cast one that wasn't a pretty good rod.

Heddons vary a little more in quality. Most of the fishermen I've talked to say the breaking point was the Black Beauty, also known as the Model 17. It sold for $35 in the 1950s and it was a good rod—Heddon's best-seller. Lesser models, like the Thoro- bred, Blue Water, and Heddon #8, are considered to be sort of ordi- nary, though still usable rods, but the top models—the Model 35 Peerless, Model 50 President, and Model 1000—are magnificent.

Those top three are easy to spot, too. They have silver hardware, usually blued, sometimes even gold plated on the Model 1000, and pretty walnut reel-seat spacers. In the mid-1950s a Model 1000 would have cost you a whopping $100. Again, in the neighborhood of a month's pay for a working stiff.

There's a long list of footnotes, fine points, and exceptions like that attached to almost all the rods you'll come across, not to mention some obscure expert somewhere who has them all memorized. For instance, Winston's fluted hollow rods weren't patented until 1951, when the patent number started appearing on the rods. If you get a Winston without the number, you know it's a pre-1951 vintage rod.

Heddon, Granger, Phillipson, and plenty of others also made hardware store rods, and dealers can often recognize them, so you'll sometimes see a listing for something like an "8½-foot, 5-weight Lyon & Coulson (probably by Heddon)." Naturally, a Heddon by any other name should cost a little less, especially since it'll probably have cheaper hardware than the name-brand rod.

I'm not as much of a Nazi about hardware as some—I don't insist on nickel silver and rare, highly figured wood spacers—but at the same time I don't think any good rods were ever made with sky blue plastic reel seats. It's hard to explain, but a rod the maker thought well of usually had a degree of class about it.

Hardware store rods have always been sort of a hard call for me. In many cases the rod companies sold their cheapest models this way, but not to outfits like Abercrombie & Fitch, which was hardly a hardware store. There are a lot of Jim Payne rods out there that say "E. F. PAYNE" on one side of the reel seat and, for instance, "ABERCROMBIE & FITCH" or "FOLSOM ARMS" on the other, and it's considered such common knowledge that the old

William Mills & Son rods were made by Leonard that some listings don't even mention it. Of course, neither the Folsom Arms
nor the A&F Paynes nor the Mills & Son Leonards are *ever*
referred to as hardware store or trade rods.

My tendency is to trust the guesses about origins and quality made by the dealers listing the rods, but you can make a fair
guess yourself about how good a rod it is by looking at the workmanship, looking at the quality of the fittings, and, most
important, by casting it.

I was just down at Mike's shop watching him clean up a
beautiful old A&F Special that was clearly made by Granger. It
has the old Granger-style nickel-silver sliding-band seat and
Coke-bottle grip, swelled butt, knurled, machined nickel-silver
ferrules that are better than I've seen on any Granger, dark,
honey-colored cane with slightly darker brown wraps, it's all
there, and it's a light, quick 9-foot 5-weight.

I was trying not to let on to Mike how much I wanted it,
but I'm afraid he knows me too well. Then again, I know rods
just well enough to understand that this one should sell for a
bit less than it would if it was a top model with the Granger
name on it.

Impregnated rods by just about any maker can be bargains
because a lot of people don't like them. They say they're too
heavy and too stiff, or that impregnation is a chintzy substitute
for a good varnish job. Some also say the dark ones are ugly,
although the same people are likely to describe a darkly flamed
rod as "richly beautiful."

I think the Wright & McGill Water Seals, the Phillipson
impregnated rods, and the Orvis Battenkills 8½ feet and shorter
for 5-weight lines are good, quick, authoritative dry-fly rods.
There are probably others, but those are the ones I know and

like. They're slightly heavier than comparable varnished rods, but the difference is in fractions of an ounce, and the extra stiffness from the impregnation seems to have been allowed for in the tapers, so the actions are nice and crisp.

I have a great little 5-weight Wright & McGill Water Seal that would have cost an impressive $75 back in the early 1950s and that came in the snazziest burgundy-and-gold anodized tube the company offered. It has a slim, reversed half Wells grip and a sweet, dry-fly action, and it's in close to mint condition. If there's one thing that's less than classy about it, it's the decal on the shaft showing a tiny little seal balancing a ball on his nose— but, after all, it *was* the 1950s.

The 9-foot impregnated rods for 6 and 7 lines are sometimes a little on the hefty side, but they're decent rods for big streamers and bass bugs and some fishermen like them as light salmon, grilse, and steelhead rods. And they're cheap. I have a nice 9-foot Water Seal that's beefy enough to cast a weight-forward 8 line. I use it for bass and—dare I say it?—carp.

As I said earlier, one-tip rods that were originally two-tip rods can be pretty cheap, but there were also any number of bamboo rods that *came* with only a single tip. Rod lists use a series of abbreviations in their descriptions to save space. The number of sections a rod has and the number of tips are designated by two numbers separated by a slash, so, for instance, a three-piece, two-tip rod is written "3/2." A two-piece rod that originally came with only one tip, like an inexpensive Orvis, will appear as "2/1—made that way." Even if it's all original and in excellent shape, a rod like that will be cheaper than a comparable two-tip rod. If you can live without the spare tip, it can be a bargain.

American collectors and fishermen don't think very highly of English rods. Maybe that's because we have an emotional investment in the split-bamboo rod being an American invention, or maybe it's because the English do tend to build things in strange, complicated, roundabout ways. (John Bradford, who's repaired a lot of English rods over the years, has an interesting analogy about how they're built; something about trying to have sex while standing up in a hammock.) Or maybe it's because some English rods *are* a little on the clunky side, with what have been described as "Continental actions."

Still, some of the lighter rods by Hardy, like the Marvels and the Phantoms, are real gems. I met a man in Alberta a few years ago who had several little Hardy dry-fly rods that were much nicer than I ever expected Hardys to be. I told him English rods were cheap in America, sent him some used-rod lists after I got home, and ended up costing him a bunch of money.

Rods by Partridge and Farlow are, by most accounts, not very good, although I *have* cast a couple of Partridge rods I thought were okay. (Not great, but okay. I never saw one I wanted to buy.)

I don't have a lot of experience with Sharps rods, but I think some of them are pretty good. My friend Mike Price has a 7½-foot rod that I built on a set of Sharps blanks about fifteen years ago. It turned out to be a 3-weight and I hardly ever used it. Finally I sold it to Mike, who fishes it with a weight-forward 4 line and thinks it's the best thing since sliced bread.

Which reminds me: Rods built from kits or put up by hobbyists on unmarked blanks are almost always cheaper than name rods, even if the workmanship is flawless and the blanks themselves are really good ones.

French rods? There are those who like the Pezon et Michelle Parabolics, and their association with the great Charles Ritz probably doesn't hurt their reputation. After all, Ritz's parabolic tapers are said to have influenced the work of both Paul Young and Jim Payne. Some kind of historic, celebrity connection like that usually helps the value of a rod, but used Pezons don't cost that much because they're, you know, *French*.

I've seen well made four- and five-sided rods that sold pretty cheaply—including some by Nat Uslan, who's famous for his five-strip rods—because, like impregnated rods, there are a fair number of fishermen who don't like them. If you *do* like them, good for you.

Now and then you'll stumble across a surprisingly fine rod by a production maker with an otherwise poor reputation, and you can often get a great deal on it because of negative name recognition. These things are fairly rare, but sometimes you can identify them by the unusually good workmanship, quality of fittings, and elaborate wraps. Horrocks-Ibbotson made a Registered Model that was surprisingly fine and so much better looking than your run-of-the-mill H-I that you have to look twice at the name. Some of the South Bend rods, like the 7½-foot Model 290s, and even some the old top-model Chubbs and Montagues, were good.

I once saw a Montague Varney (made by George Varney under his own name at Montague) that had fancy, elaborate silk wraps, all-silver hardware, and a widely swelled butt with rosewood inserts between the cane splines. It was a beautiful, romantic-looking old 9-foot, 4-weight rod that, because it was ostensibly a Montague, cost the owner not much more than pocket change.

Now, a lot of the older bamboo fly rods were designed for wet-fly casting with silk lines, and for most of us they just don't get it for day-to-day fishing, although it's fun to fish with silk lines and borderline antique rods now and then just to see how things used to be and to prove to any of your friends who may have begun to doubt it that you really are twisted. I mean, being considered a nut by some fly fishers because you use bamboo rods is one thing, but being thought of as nuts by other bamboo rod fanatics is something only a dedicated few can accomplish.

The reel seats on many of these old rods are full-metal cap-and-ring affairs and they're usually noticeably longer than more modern reel seats. Lots of older rods also have grips of sheet cork fitted over shaped wooden handles, or grips made of thinner cork rings than you'll see on modern rods. Many of them came on fitted wood form cases that fit into canvas bags. Lots of cases have survived, but it's rare to find one still in the bag. I think the bags either were lost or got wet and have long since rotted away, probably taking some of the rods with them.

Some are perfectly good rods that happen to have actions we don't appreciate anymore and others just have poor actions, period. Some of them are nameless or "unmarked," either because they lost their names to a refinish job somewhere in the past or, in some cases, because they were so cheap no one wanted to take responsibility for them.

Still, some of them are surprisingly good—especially the shorter rods and those made up into the 1930s and 1940s—and I mean good by modern standards, using modern lines.

My friend Mike Sinclair knows more about these old pro-duction and trade rods than anyone I've ever talked to. He does a good job of identifying and dating nameless rods, but even he has trouble telling the good ones from the bad ones just by looking at them. He says the consistency of a lot of these rods varied widely, and he's not sure if the good ones were mistakes or if they represent those days at the factory when they actually did it right. "You just have to get your hands on them and cast them," he says.

I guess that's what it always comes down to. The rods I've talked about here are just a sampling of the ones that sometimes turn up for sale. The more of them you see and cast, the more likely you'll be to stumble on the rods that really speak to you, and it can be funny which ones those turn out to be. I think I have about as many favorite rods as I do good friends—a precious few of each—and both the rods and the people are a pretty mixed bag. A few would probably impress anyone right off the bat. The rest you'd have to get to know.

The one thing I've learned is that the price of a rod doesn't necessarily reflect its real value.

I'll never forget the day I got to cast a real, by God, 8-foot, 6-weight Garrison. It was the first genuinely classic rod I'd ever gotten my hands on and when I walked out on the owner's lawn with it and began to cast, I thought the sky would open up, a shaft of light would descend, and everything would suddenly become clear. What became clear was that I was casting a perfectly serviceable 6-weight rod, maybe a little on the slow side for my taste.

I've heard this same story from other fishermen and I think the legends attached to some of these great, classic rods, plus their scarceness and their huge price tags, can set you up to be a little disappointed. You can appreciate the rod and even be damned impressed by it, but there's a moment when you realize it could never be as good as you've been led to expect.

And then there's another moment when you have to wonder if maybe it's just you. Marty Keane once wrote that those of us who don't fully appreciate Garrison rods may be "like some amateur violinist with a Stradivarius," and that we are "unequal to the challenge of the instrument." Yeah, maybe. I mean, how can you argue with that?

Still, I remember thinking (and meaning no disrespect, either) that for what that Garrison would cost, I could buy a stack of good Grangers and fish them for two weeks in British Columbia.

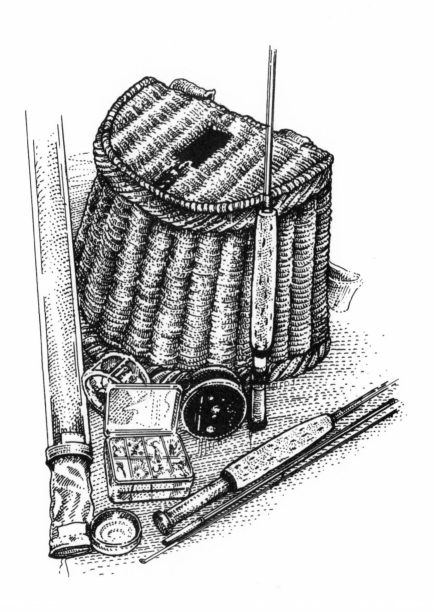

6

Odds and Ends

TAKING CARE OF a bamboo rod is pretty simple, but important. The old E. F. Payne Rod Company label says, "BE SURE THAT BOTH YOUR ROD AND CLOTH CASE ARE THOROUGHLY DRY BEFORE PUTTING AWAY IN ALU-MINUM CASE OR OTHER CONTAINER. DAMPNESS RESULTS IN MILDEW THAT WILL RUIN A ROD—AND WE CANNOT BE RESPON-SIBLE FOR DAMAGE RESULTING FROM SUCH TREATMENT." That seems clear enough.

It's a good idea to wipe a rod down with a dry cloth before you put it in the tube after a day of fishing, even if it doesn't seem wet, and I make a habit of air-drying my rod overnight after I get home. I'll lay it out on a table in the back room on top of the rod bag and put it back in the tube the next morning. And yes, it helps that Colorado is a semi-arid climate.

If I'm camping or at a lodge where I don't want to leave my rod lying around in the open, I'll wipe it off well and store it in the tube with the cap off. That's not ideal, but it lets the rod air out a little and it beats having the camp cook set a hot coffeepot on it. A few years ago A. K. and I fished in a pouring rain in Labrador for a week. Our rods wouldn't have gotten much wetter if we'd tied rocks to them and sunk them in the lake, and storing them uncapped at the camp worked fine, especially with six other fishermen, four guides, and a cook milling around, although we air-dried them for several days when we got home.

By the way, if you store a rod in the tube with the cap off, try not to lose the cap.

Inspecting the rods after a trip has become a ritual with me ever since I ruined one by not automatically going through the motions. I didn't bother looking at the rod because I'd carried it on the trip but I'd never used it. It never occurred to me that in the course of sitting in several drift boats on three rivers in two Canadian provinces, some water had seeped into the case, probably around the bottom cap. By the time I took the rod out a month later, it was black and rotten and it stank like a dead sucker.

It wasn't a very expensive rod, but it was a good one that would have had a lifetime of fishing left in it if it hadn't been owned by an idiot.

It's also best to keep your rods away from heat, which includes direct sunlight shinning through a window—either at home or in the car—woodstoves, hot-air vents, and so on. Heat can soften the varnish, loosen the glue, and do all kinds of unpleasant things to a rod.

I store my rods in their cases and so do most of the people I know, but John Bradford suggests that you store rods in the off season by hanging them in the back of a closet in the bags only. (If the bags don't have loops on them, use safety pins.) John says it's cool and dry in the closet and if someone breaks in to steal your rods, they might end up with nothing but empty cases.

When you're taking a rod out of the tube, slide the whole thing out in the bag while making a ring with your thumb and forefinger to keep from banging the guides against the side of the tube. That's especially important with older rods that came in small-diameter, snug-fitting tubes. Modern tubes are roomier, but sometimes they're so big they let the rod rattle around inside.

Do the same in reverse when you're putting it away—make a ring with your fingers and don't bang the guides—and always store the spare tip in the bag and in the tube while you're fishing.

I think it was Marty Keane who said you should always put your rod away first at the end of the day, before you take off your waders, pour a cup of coffee from the thermos, or anything else. Most of the people I fish with do that and I think it's a good habit to get into. Broken rods are like hunting accidents: More than half happen back at the pickup.

John Bradford says that if you *must* lean your rod anywhere while you're searching for your keys, put it against the windshield on the driver's side with the reel seat under the windshield wiper. If you can forget it there, you deserve whatever happens.

I'll add a footnote: Scratch that if you're going to be putting a boat on the roof.

It's also a good idea to look around the car—including on the roof—one last time before you get in and drive to the nearest café. Maybe you were so worried about getting your rod put away you left your reel on the bumper.

When you put a rod together, hold the pieces with your hands close to the ferrules, line up the guides, and seat the ferrules straight together. Some rods have what are called "witness marks" on the ferrules, which are a big help. If the marks are lined up right, so are the sections; you don't even have to sight down the rod to check, although you probably will anyway.

Never twist the ferrules. Twisting stresses a bamboo rod in a direction it wasn't made to be stressed and several ugly things can happen, all of which can lead to a broken rod, either right now or eventually. If the guides don't quite line up, pull the rod apart and try again. Do the same thing in reverse when you're taking it apart. Pull straight, don't twist.

When you're taking a rod down, it's okay to grab it with your hands a little farther apart, just be careful not to bend the rod or twist it. Tom Clark has a little mantra for this: "Rod together, hands together. Rod apart, hands apart."

Now and then you'll get a stuck ferrule, and nine times out of ten the solution to that is a set of ferrule pullers: two pads of clean, soft inner-tube rubber, one in each hand, to let you get a good grip on the rod. I know, it doesn't seem like it would make that much difference, but John Bradford told me about this years ago and it's been the answer ever since. There are two things that are always in the back pouch of my fishing vest: dry matches and ferrule pullers.

If you don't have ferrule pullers, try drying the rod and your hands. It can also help to warm your hands in your pockets for a few minutes. Most stuck ferrules aren't really stuck, it's just that you can't get a good hold on the rod.

There are those who say you should give your ferrules a light coat of hard (not soft) beeswax or paraffin to keep them from sticking, although you should avoid the traditional earwax, nose grease, or anything with a petroleum base. Others say no, you should seat ferrules dry. After all, ferrules are made of nickel silver in part because it won't stick to itself, and anything you put on ferrules will pick up grit that will eventually abrade them.

For what it's worth, I keep my ferrules clean and seat them dry, but I'm not prepared to defend that to the death. If your favorite rod guru tells you to grease your ferrules, then grease 'em with my blessing.

The one use I've found for hard wax is, it will temporarily tighten up ferrules that have gotten so loose the tip section twists or starts to unseat when you cast the rod. The final solution is to have the rod referruled, but a little paraffin will let you limp it through another season or two.

Everyone agrees that you should clean your ferrules, but naturally there's some disagreement about how to do that. Some say you should clean ferrules with Formula 409 cleaner or acetone (use a rag for the male ferrule and a Q-tip for the female); others say just use a dry, coarse rag.

I've heard rod makers and restorers say that if your ferrules are lightly tarnished you can clean them with fine steel wool, but then there are those like Mike Sinclair, who recently wrote, "NEVER, NEVER, NEVER try to eliminate a sticking problem by cleaning the ferrules with ANY abrasive." That's probably good advice.

If you're ever in doubt about ferrules or anything else, call someone who knows before you do anything. And I mean *anything*.

When you're playing a big fish on a bamboo rod, try not to do it entirely off the tip. I've heard it said that you should turn the rod over now and then with a big fish on to equalize the stress on the tip, but I'm usually way too excited to think of that, and even when I do it seems too awkward. I just try to point the rod down toward the fish a little more and play him off the butt.

I guess that's more important with light little rods than with heavier ones, but if you use a favorite bamboo rod a lot you'll probably get sets in the tips sooner or later. (Actually, some of my best fishing trips were the ones where I came home with my rods a little bent.) A good rod maker can straighten a section with heat, but that's the kind of ticklish operation that will wreck the rod if it's done wrong. Don't try it yourself.

I understand it's possible to fish the life right out of a bamboo fly rod, but I've never done that, although God knows I've tried. I've been fishing hard with my 8½-foot, 5-weight Mike Clark rod for long enough to have had Mike straighten both tips two or three times and it's still fine. I once asked him how much longer this could go on. He said, "We'll see."

Actually, after many years of use a bamboo rod can develop a new "spine," and a good rod restorer can rewrap the guides accordingly and it'll probably be good as new.

Several people who should know have told me it's a good idea to polish your rod every now and then with a light furniture wax to clean it and to keep the varnish from drying out. Mike Clark recommends that, but John Bradford says the wax is just as likely to eventually soften the varnish, so it's better to simply wipe the rod off with a damp rag, then dry it with a dry rag.

That's just one of the many things competent rod builders disagree on.

Beyond that, just fish the rod and try not to abuse it. When you hook your fly in a bush, don't yank on it with the tip. When you put the rod away, don't bang the ferrules on the bottom of the tube; that can hurt both the ferrules themselves and the bamboo shafts. Don't use the rod tube as a walking stick for the same reason. (By the way, a bamboo rod should go into the tube with the ferrules pointed down, except for those few rods that come with ferrule plugs looped to the top of the bag. In that case, the reel-seat end of the butt section *has* to go down.) Don't slam it in a car door, step on it, or lend it to a clumsy friend. Bamboo fly rods aren't as delicate or as complicated as some people seem to think, but they're not idiotproof, either.

Over the years I've tried lots of different fly lines on bamboo rods—not all of them, but lots—and I've finally settled on the old peach-colored Cortland 444s. I like them because they're supple, they hold up pretty well under hard use (they hold up even better if you clean them now and then), and they've been around more or less unchanged since the mid-1960s, which means they haven't been improved out of existence and I've been able to get used to them.

(Mike Clark prefers the Scientific Anglers Ultra lines—just to show we don't agree on everything.)

Of course, just about any good fly line will work on a bamboo rod, and it's not hard to find a fly fisher who'll say he can't tell much difference between one line and another. Still, I think bamboo rods like the softer, more supple lines better than the hard, stiff ones.

I also think most bamboo rods perform best at their normal casting ranges with double-taper lines, and many makers design their tapers with DT lines in mind. Line-weight designations almost always refer to double-taper lines, and if there are two numbers, the second will mean a weight-forward. A "5-weight" rod casts a DT5 line and a "5/6-weight" casts either a DT5 or a WF6.

Except for Orvis rods. For years now, Orvis has rated its rods for weight-forward lines, so a 5-weight Orvis is, nine times out of ten, really a 4-weight. I don't know why they do that.

Then again, lots of good old rods—from Paynes and Garrisons to Grangers—came without any line designation at all. These things date back to the good old days when rod makers allowed as how different fishermen had different casting styles and figured you'd be smart enough to decide which line you liked best on one of their rods.

You'll see people put rods like that together, wiggle them a few times, and confidently say something like, "This is a 6-weight." I've done that myself and I've even been right a few times, but if I actually take that rod out and cast it with a variety of lines between, say a DT5 and a WF7, I might have to change my opinion a little.

Sometimes model numbers will give you a clue to line weight, although often it's *just* a clue. Nine-foot Granger fly rods came in at least four model designations: 9043, 9050, 9052, and 9053, weighing 4¾, 5, 5½, and 5¾ ounces respectively. (According to the 1941 catalog, those weights "do not include the extra weight of the locking screw reel seat," which adds about ½ ounce.) The model numbers and weights weren't on the rods themselves, but they were on the labels on the original cases. I think the two lower model numbers are 5-weights and the two higher ones are 6/7-weights, but I've never seen an official line designation for a Granger rod either on the rod itself, on the label, or in any of the old catalogs.

I have an idiosyncrasy when it comes to lines. I almost always fish my 4-weight rods with a weight-forward 5 line, and my 5-weights with a DT5. That's because I usually use the 4-weights on small mountain streams where the casts are short. A weight-forward line has more weight out front and loads the rod better at short ranges. As I said, it's an idiosyncrasy. The older you get, the more of those you'll have.

Speaking of which, every once in a while I get on a jag and do some fishing with silk lines, usually on older rods that were designed for them, but sometimes on newer ones, too.

Modern plastic-coated lines didn't appear until the early 1950s and silk lines were commonly in use up until then—well *past* then by holdouts who were suspicious of the newfangled plastic jobs. A silk line is slightly thinner, slightly heavier, and a lot more supple than a modern line, so you can imagine how luxurious and effortless it is to cast, and you can also see why the guides on fly rods used to be noticeably smaller than they are now.

Many of the bamboo rods I've tried them on actually cast better with silk lines than with modern ones, but silk lines are sort of a logistical nightmare. You have to stop several times in a day to dry them and re-dress them (or carry a second line for the evening rise), you should spool them off the reel and store them dry on a line winder to keep them from rotting, and eventually they'll begin to lose their oil and varnish finish, so you'll have to refinish them.

To refinish a silk line, you have to first wash it in hot water and detergent, then rinse it in plain hot water, and then dry it bone dry, first between newspapers or paper towels, then in the air. If it's still tacky, wash it and dry it again. This winter I resurrected an old, sticky line that took a dozen baths over a week or so before it was down to the bare silk. A few days into it I began to wonder if it was worth the trouble, but you know how it is when you start something. Next time I'll look for a line that's in better shape to begin with.

Eventually the line will be clean, but it'll also be dry and rough, so you have to polish it using a dry cloth and a very, very mild abrasive like talcum powder or tooth powder (an ancestor of toothpaste, still available in drugstores run by old, gray-haired guys.) Polish the line until it's silky smooth and then re-dress it with Mucilin line dressing in the red can. This can take many coats, and I think it's best done outside on a hot, sunny day. If it's too cool, the Mucilin hardens and won't sink into the line.

Everyone I've talked to says to use only the Mucilin that comes in the *red* can, not the green one. Green Mucilin—like most line dressings—has silicone in it, and silicone isn't good for silk lines. Red Mucilin is mostly animal fat. It's still made in England and it's about as easy to find as tooth powder.

Silk lines are great for people who really enjoy fussing with their tackle. I fish with them every now and then, usually on slow-paced days close to home when stringing my line between two trees to dry and taking a nap sounds like a pretty good idea. Most days I'm in more of a plastic-line kind of mood, but every now and then. . . .

A man named Noel Buxton is still making silk fly lines in England. They go by the brand name of Phoenix and they're being imported by Len Codella at Heritage Sporting Collectibles. These lines are handmade of pure silk and hand finished with various oils and varnishes, no doubt mixed to an ancient, secret formula. There are around five hours of handwork in each line, plus as much as six to eight weeks of drying time. The lines retail for about $200 apiece but, as Len recently pointed out to me, a good silk line, properly used and cared for, will last you twenty years, while a modern plastic line will start to give out after about two seasons and there's nothing you can do except buy a new one for $50. That means that in the same twenty years you'll spend $500 on modern lines—assuming the price doesn't go up, which is a damned rash assumption.

Still, two hundred bucks is a lot for a fly line. The silk lines I use are all old ones, although three of them were still new in the box when I got them: two Newtons and a Sakatak from Von Lengerke & Antoine. Some were just given to me by people who had them lying around and didn't know what to do with them, one came on an old reel, and the one I actually bought— an unused Newton HDH—cost something like $10 or $20. Silk lines in decent shape are hard to find, but if you do find one it'll be pretty cheap.

The Newton isn't all *that* old, because it gives the old letter designation, "HDH," plus "NEW CODE DT6." That's unusual. Most just give the letters. Here are the translations:

IGI	=	DT3	IGJ	=	WF3
HFH	=	DT4	HFG	=	WF4
HEH	=	DT5	HEG	=	WF5
HDH	=	DT6	HDG	=	WF6
HCH	=	DT7	HCF	=	WF7
GBG	=	DT8	GBF	=	WF8
GAG	=	DT9	GAF	=	WF9
GAAG	=	DT10	GAAF	=	WF10
GAAAG	=	DT11	GAAAF	=	WF11
GAAAAG	=	DT12	GAAAAF	=	WF12

You'll often see an older rod marked something like, "HCH OR D." Single letters designate "level" lines—that is, lines that are the same diameter from one end to the other. Level lines don't cast anywhere near as well as tapered ones, which is why you don't see them anymore. The best use I've found for level silk lines is, they look neat on old reels used as paperweights.

Speaking of reels, there's a big temptation to put a sexy one on a fine bamboo rod. You know, one of those historic-looking internal-spool jobs with the serpentine, counterbalanced handles and black side plates. A well-made, finely balanced, smooth-running reel is a sweet device, it'll look cool on your rod, and, if you fish long and hard enough, the day will come when it really will help you land a God-awful big fish you probably would have lost with a cheaper reel.

There are good new ones around—Bob Corsetti's Peerless reels, Carpenter and Caseys, Robichauds, Sarciones, and some others. There are Stanley Bogdan reels if you can get one and afford it (I've seen some Bogdans, but I've never owned one), there are Hardy Perfects with their ball bearings and solid side plates (they're still made) and older, similar Hardys like the Uniquas, plus the good old Zwargs, vom Hofes, and all the others you'll end up knowing about if you get bit by reels.

Collectors, and people who lean a little in that direction, sometimes want to have a "period" reel on an old rod. That can amount to a drop in the bucket if you want to put an old brass Pflueger Progress on a Chubb, or it can double the price of a four-figure rig if you feel you need a Bogdan on your Payne. It's like fishing a silk line on a rod made back when silk was the standard: It's not necessary, maybe not even a good idea for day-to-day fishing, but it does make a kind of sense.

A lot of fishermen like a slightly heavier reel on a bamboo rod to balance it properly, and heavy doesn't necessarily mean expensive, either. The old American-made Pflueger Medalists are plenty hefty, a good one should cost you less than a new plastic fly line, and it'll be historically correct on something like a newer Granger, Heddon, or Phillipson.

Be careful buying old reels—or even new ones, for that matter—because all reels do not necessarily fit all reel seats. Try the reel before you buy it or tell the dealer you'll return it if it doesn't fit your rod.

There are two schools of thought on balance: One says it matters, the other says it doesn't. I agree that the balance point of a rod fitted with its reel should be right under your thumb on the cork grip, but I've never lost sleep over it and I've never bought a new reel just to move the balance point of a rod an inch or two.

On the other hand, I *have* heard of fishermen gluing lead shot in the frames of their reels to add weight for balance. That seems a little extreme to me (although it's not the weirdest thing I've ever heard of fishermen doing), but why not if they think it matters and it makes them happy?

I mean, that's why some of us use bamboo fly rods and, as far as that goes, why we fish at all: because we think it matters and it makes us happy.

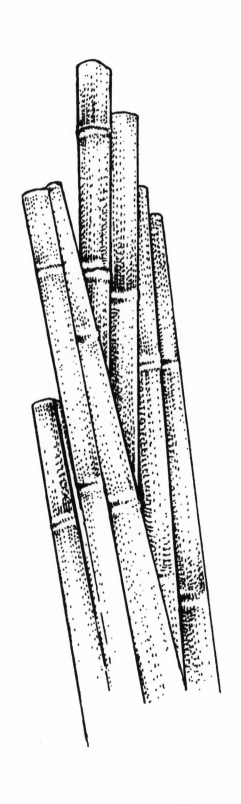

Bibliography

Here are a few books and a magazine that will be helpful if you're interested in buying or learning about bamboo fly rods, and a few you should read if you're interested in building rods.

The Angler's Bamboo by Luis Marden. Lyons & Burford, 1997.

The Angler's Workshop by Letcher Lambuth. Champoeg Press, 1979.

The Bamboo Flyrod by Claude M. Kreider. Macmillan Co., 1951.

The Best of the Planing Form by R. L. Barch and Robert McKeon. Alder Creek Enterprises, 1997.

Bamboo Rod Restoration Handbook by Michael Sinclair. Centennial Publications, 1994.

Classic Bamboo Rodmakers Past and Present by Dick Spurr. Centennial Publications, 1992.

Classic Rods and Rodmakers by Martin J. Keane. Classic Publishing Company, 1976.

Colorado Classic Cane by Dick Spurr and Michael Sinclair. Centennial Publications, 1991.

Dickerson, The Man and his Rods by Gerald S. Stein and Jim Schaaf. Centennial Publications, 1991.

The Fine Bamboo Fly Rod by Stuart Kirkfield. Stackpole Books, 1986.

Fishing Rods by Divine by Michael Sinclair. Centennial Publications, 1993.

Great Fishing Tackle Catalogs of the Golden Age edited by Samuel Melner and Hermann Kessler. Lyons & Burford, 1989.

Handcrafting Bamboo Fly Rods by Wayne Cattanach. W. Cattanach Rod Co., 1992.

Heddon: The Rod with the Fighting Heart by Michael Sinclair. Centennial Publications, 1997.

How to Make Bamboo Fly Rods by George W. Barnes. Winchester Press, 1977.

The Idyll of Split Bamboo by Dr. George Parker Holden. Stewart & Kidd, 1920.

A Master's Guide to Building a Bamboo Fly Rod by Everett Garrison and Hoagy B. Carmichael. Meadow Run Press, 1994.

The Planing Form newsletter, Ron Barch, editor. P.O. Box 365, Hastings, MI 49058.

The Sporting Craftsmen by Art Carter. Countrysport Press, 1994.

Trout Tackle—Two by Ernest Schwiebert. E. P. Dutton, 1984.

Wes Jordan: Profile of a Rodmaker by Dick Spurr and Gloria Jordan. Centennial Publications, 1992.

Appendices

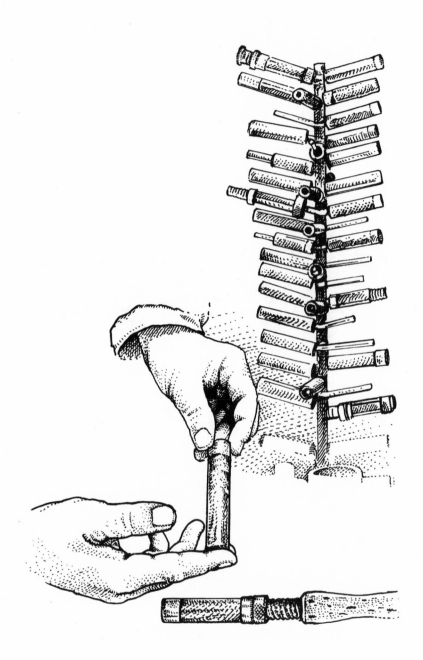

Appendix I

Bamboo Rod Dealers

Bamboo Broker
(new bamboo fly rods)
2041 South 380th Street
Federal Way, WA 98003

The Cane Clinic
(used rods and restorations)
Mike Sinclair
2100 Blake Street
Denver, CO 80205

W. E. Carpenter Rod Co.
Box 405
Chester, NY 10918

Thomas H. Clark
1308 West Washington
Jackson, MI 49203

The Classic Chronicle
Dick Spurr
256 Nashua Court
Grand Junction, CO 81503

Classic Rods & Tackle, Inc.
Martin J. Keane
P.O. Box 288
Ashley Falls, MA 01222

Heritage Sporting Collectibles
Len Codella
2201 South Carnegie Drive
Inverness, FL 34450

The Jordan-Mills Rod Co.
Carmine Lisella
11 Wesley Road
Congers, NY 10920

John J. McGrath
4137 Hidden Oaks Road
Santa Barbara, CA 93105

Andy Sekora and Bill McRoy
3626 Theisen Road
Gaylord, MI 49735

Rods & Reels
Bob Corsetti
17 Massasoit Road
Nashua, NH 03063

Appendix II

Bamboo Rod Makers

As well as making new rods, some of these craftsmen also do repairs and restorations and may now and then deal in used rods.

Marc Aroner
P.O. Box 81
Conway, MA 01341

Glen Brackett
R. L. Winston
Drawer T
Twin Bridges, MT 59754

John Bradford
3700 Lawndale
Fort Worth, TX 76133

Per Brandin
10254 San Pablo Avenue
El Cerrito, CA 94530

C. W. "Sam" Carlson
Route 31, P.O. Box 322
Greenville, NH 03048

Hoagy B. Carmichael
Crosby Road
North Salem, NY 10560

W. E. Carpenter
Box 52
Huntington Mills, PA 18622

W. Cattanach Rod Co.
15315 Apple Avenue
Casnovia, MI 49318

Mike Clark
South Creek, Ltd.
P.O. Box 981
Lyons, CO 80540

DiCicco Custom Fly Rods
c/o Scheffield Custom Tackle
1107 Fairlane Drive
Auquippa, PA 15001

Tom Dorsey
Thomas & Thomas
2 Avenue A
Turner Falls, MA 01376

Douglas J. Duck
3821 Hollow Creek Road
Fort Worth, TX 76116

Ed Fody
1109 Delmar Avenue
Franklin Square, NY 11010

J. W. Gallas Rod Co.
7 Mirijo Road
Danbury, CT 06811

Robert Gorman
Green River Rodmakers
Box 817, Rural Route 4
Brattleboro, VT 05301

Leon F. Hanson
1566 Nantucket
Plymouth, MI 48170

Hardy USA
10 Godwin Place
Midland Park, NJ 07432

G. H. Howells
655 33rd Street
Richmond, CA 94804

C. W. Jenkins Rod Co.
5735 South Jericho Way
Aurora, CO 80015

H. L. Jennings
3050 Richmond Drive
Colorado Springs, CO 80922

Dave Klausmeyer
P.O. Box 105
Steuben, ME 04680

Doug Kulick
Kane Klassics
P.O. Box 8124
Freemont, CA 94537

Ron Kusse
Rena Marie Circle
Washington, NY 10992

R. W. Lancaster
11685 McKee Road
North Huntingdon, PA 15642

H. L. Leonard Rod Company
2 Oak Street
P.O. Box 2797
Kennebunkport, ME 04046

F. D. Lyons
7156 Southeast 118th Drive
Portland, OR 97266

Dave Male
Camden Valley
Shushan, NY 12873

Timothy P. Marchetti
103 Washington Street
Camden, ME 04843

George Maurer
Sweet Water Rods
151 Sutter Road
Lenhartsville, PA 19534

Orvis Company
Route 7A
Manchester, VT 05254

John Parker
245 East Line Road
Ballston Lake, NY 12019

Partridge of Redditch
Mount Pleasant
Redditch, Worchestershire
B97 4JE England

The Powell Rod Co.
P.O. Box 4000
Chico, CA 95927

Rangeley Rod Co.
P.O. Box 1270
Rangeley, ME 04970

Joe Sarcione
P.O. Box 372
Sandy, OR 97055

Jim Schaaf
P.O. Box 535
Concord, CA 94522

D. G. Schroeder
3822 Brunswick Lane
Janesville, WI 53546

Sharps Rods
Doug Brewer Fly Fishing
P.O. Box 699
Florence, MT 59833

M. K. Spittler
4119 Columbus Avenue South
Minneapolis, MN 55407

R. W. Summers
90 River Road East
Traverse City, MI 49684

R. D. Taylor
P.O. Box L
Hobart, NY 13788-0412

A. J. Thramer
645 Powers, Unit C
Eugene, OR 97402

Art Weiler
313 East Street
Bound Brook, NJ 08805

Daryll Whitehead
611 Northwest 48th Street
Seattle, WA 98107

Mario Wojnicki
10254 San Pablo Avenue
El Cerrito, CA 94530

Max Yerxa
P.O. Box 266
Colusa, CA 95932

Todd Young
Paul H. Young Co.
535 West Front Street
Traverse City, MI 49684

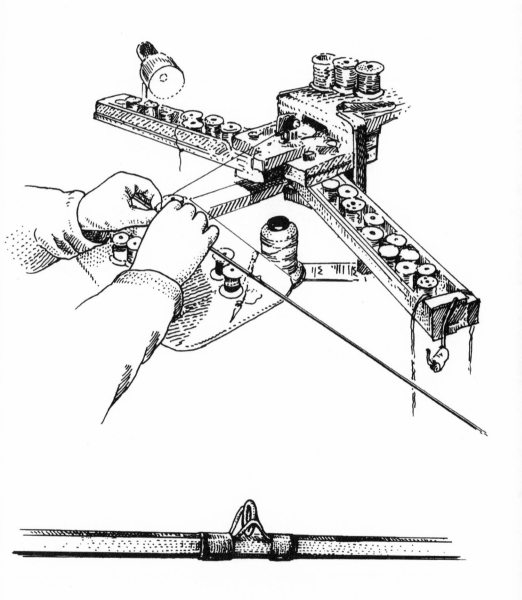